POEMS
FOR EVERY
EMOTION

YOU'RE
NEVER
TOO
MUCH

CHARLIE
CASTELLETTI

FIRST INK

FIRST INK

First published 2025 by First Ink,
an imprint of Pan Macmillan
The Smithson, 6 Briset Street, London EC1M 5NR
EU representative: Macmillan Publishers Ireland Ltd, 1st Floor,
The Liffey Trust Centre, 117–126 Sheriff Street Upper, Dublin 1 D01 YC43
Associated companies throughout the world

ISBN 978-1-0350-7022-0

1 3 5 7 9 8 6 4 2

A CIP catalogue record for this book is available from the British Library.

Printed and bound in the UK using 100% Renewable Electricity by CPI Group (UK) Ltd

MIX
Paper | Supporting
responsible forestry
FSC® C116313

Visit **www.panmacmillan.com** to read more about all our books and buy them.

To Lola, you inspire me

Contents

Introduction xvii

Why Attie Lime xix

Raw thoughts on 'too much' Christina Alejandra xxi

I'm Feeling . . . in Love 1

Waffle House Crush Harry Josephine Giles 3

O, Were I Loved As I Desire to Be! Alfred, Lord Tennyson 4

enemies to lovers trope Kelsey Day 5

Two Boys in the Dark Charlie Brodie 7

The perfect caress has a velocity of
three centimetres per second Jack Cooper 9

I Wish in the City of Your Heart Robley Wilson 10

By-Product Aaron Cawood 11

I loved you first: but afterwards
your love Christina Rossetti 12

Valentine Carol Ann Duffy 13

Text Carol Ann Duffy 15

I'm Feeling . . . Angry 17

Red Shauna Darling
Robertson 19

Betrayal Claire Schlinkert 20

This Be The Verse Philip Larkin 21

Charcuterie   Annabelle Cormack   22
Enough   David Ly   24
When I argue, I forget to be me(ek)   Deborah Finding   25
For When You Need Validation
    For Your Anger   Nikita Gill   26
A Poison Tree   William Blake   27
from Poem about My Rights   June Jordan   28
Happy New Year   Harry Josephine Giles   29
Too Angry   Charlie Castelletti   30

I'm Feeling . . . Heart/Broken   33
little recipe   Dide   35
If I can stop one Heart from
    breaking   Emily Dickinson   36
One Minute with Lavender   LJ Ireton   37
Wreckages   Aaron Cawood   39
Almost Feelings   Nikita Gill   40
Little Heartbreak   Wilhelmina Stitch   41
What I've Learned From
    Heartbreak   Nadine Aisha Jassat   42
After   Tracie Renee   43
Heartbreak Echoes   Tim Stobierski   45
Let it let you let them go   Pan Saville   46

I'm Feeling . . . Overwhelmed, Anxious, or Like I'm Too Much

I'm Feeling . . . Overwhelmed, Anxious, or Like I'm Too Much — 49

Grasping	Shauna Darling Robertson	51
Knot	Rob Walton	52
The Anxiety List	Lois Foster	54
The Healing List	Lois Foster	56
I WANT ! TO WANT ! TO LIVE !	Despy Boutris	58
Natural Buoyancy	Philip Waddell	59
Jack-in-the-Box	Rosamund Taylor	60
Portrait of My Anxiety as an Imp	Rosamund Taylor	62
Trans Anxiety	Aidan Summers	63
Hypocrite	Charlotte Moore	64
Wildfires burn across Australia as Edward Cullen takes his shirt off for the twentieth time	Elspeth Wilson	65
Poetry Submission	Christina Hennemann	68
Overshare	Annabelle Cormack	69
Anxiety	Casper E. Falls	71
You're Never Too . . .	Laura Mucha	73

I'm Feeling . . . Hopeful — 75

Small Green Thing	John McCullough	77
Hope	Cat Winters	78
Glossary for Hope	Munira Tabassum Ahmed	80
Good News	Carl Burkitt	81

Today is a good day   Elizabeth Gibson   82

Small Kindnesses   Danusha Laméris   83

"Hope" is the thing with feathers   Emily Dickinson   84

Because the World Didn't End   Cal Brantley   85

The First Cosmonaut   Dom Conlon   87

When You Ask Me If I Can Say   Rosemerry Wahtola
    Yes to the World as It Is   Trommer   89

Finish Lines   Emma Hutson   90

If I Can't   Julie Stevens   92

This Too Will Pass   Grace Noll Crowell   93

I Am Alone   Carmella de Keyser   94

I'm Feeling . . . Reminiscent

    97

The Sunflower Sonnets   Dale Booton   99

Me and G #1 Grandpa   Stewart Ennis   101

Walking in the Arboretum at Night   Rainie Oet   103

Deep Dish   Peter Scalpello   104

A Thunderstorm in Town   Thomas Hardy   106

'I Thought of You'   Sara Teasdale   107

Blackberries   Dredhëza Maloku   108

Sometimes . . .   Emma Perry   110

Eulogy   Emmy Clarke   112

Later   Emmy Clarke   113

It's only a number   Jer Hayes   114

24 hour Tesco   Jo Morris Dixon   115

you.again   Tom Flanagan   116

I'm Feeling . . . Joyful   121

For the Guy Who Keeps Telling
   Me to Smile   *Lisa Varchol Perron*   123
The Orange   *Wendy Cope*   124
Shining Things   *Elizabeth Gould*   125
I Am Carrying Happiness   *Maria Jastrzębska*   126
Happiness, as a Dress   *Hannah Linden*   128
The Best Medicine   *Gregory Woods*   130
What a Joy It Is   *Harry Woodgate*   132
Don't Hesitate   *Mary Oliver*   134

I'm Feeling . . . Fearful, or Insecure   137

What Will Become of Me?   *Raye Halabuza*   139
Profile Picture Insecurity   *Sarah Peters*   140
I Am Trying   *Aaron Cawood*   141
Fear has me frozen   *Charlie Morris*   142
Mask   *Mark Bird*   144
Fear   *Sara Teasdale*   145
An Octopus Dwells Inside My
   Head   *Cat Winters*   146
Post   *Matthew Freeman*   147
What I Heard Her Say   *Rosemerry Wahtola*
                        Trommer   148
if nothing else   *Harry Woodgate*   149
Here's what I'm afraid of   *Charlie Castelletti*   151
The Ones Who Doubt You
   and The Ones Who Don't   *Nikita Gill*   153

I'm Feeling . . . Blue 155

Today Will Be Mostly Blue	Sue Hardy-Dawson	157
Dissociation Is a Mental Process of Disconnecting from One's Thoughts, Feelings, Memories or Surroundings	Shauna Darling Robertson	158
The Blues	Langston Hughes	159
The Depression Trail	Karl Knights	160
Internet Friendship	Betty Doyle	163
Breaking Down the Blues	Daniel Galef	166
I felt a Funeral, in my Brain	Emily Dickinson	168
Away Message	MJ Huntsgood	169
Poem for a Pebble	Victoria Gatehouse	170
Sad	Annabelle Sami	172
That Time of the Month Again	M. Stevenson	173

I'm Feeling . . . Grief 175

I measure every Grief I meet	Emily Dickinson	177
Love/Loss	Jamie Pacton	179
~ on grief ~	Cora Dessalines	180
Echo	Christina Rossetti	182
Grief	Lysz Flo	183
The Night Where You No Longer Live	Meghan O'Rourke	185
The Three Deaths	C. T. Wood	187
The Debt	Paul Laurence Dunbar	189
On Landing and Leaving Home	Dredhëza Maloku	190
Remember	Christina Rossetti	192

I'm Feeling . . . Lost or Confused, or Like I Need Help   195

An Ordinary Day	Norman MacCaig	197
There's No One Else Like Me	Barbara Bleiman	199
Elemental	Clara Elena García	201
Loss and Gain	Henry Wadsworth Longfellow	202
Not So Dear Diary	Kate Williams	203
Age Fourteen, Online Quiz	Despy Boutris	204
A learned man came to me once	Stephen Crane	207
The Bully	Lucy Burke	208
At Low Tide	Christina Gessler	211
Good Listener	Stephen Lightbown	212
Crew	Eleanor Powell	213
Take Care	Joshua Seigal	216
Subtext	Sarah Ziman	217

I'm Feeling . . . In Need of Your Wisdom   219

felt	Stewart Ennis	221
Message to the 14-Year-Old Me	Brian Bilston	222
Sensitive	Raye Halabuza	223
Love and Friendship	Emily Brontë	224
A Love Letter	Raven Wildwood	225
A Golden Shovel At Heartbreak Hotel	Jen Feroze	227
Leaving the Tate	Fleur Adcock	228
Lemons	Rob Walton	230
The Whole Oak	Imogen Russell Williams	231

This Is a Shout Out   Shauna Darling
     Robertson   232

On Her Fifteenth Birthday, I Tell
     My Sister Why a Woman is Like
     a Bouquet of Flowers   Megan J. Arlett   233
Show Them   Annabelle Sami   234
Bring a Coat   Charlotte Moore   236
Life   Paul Laurence Dunbar   237

Index of First Lines   239
Index of Poets and Translators   247
Copyright Acknowledgements   253
Editor's Acknowledgements   259

Introduction

It is almost serendipitous, but I am writing this at a time in my life when I feel simultaneously like I'm too much and yet not enough for the world – and so this has been the perfect project to get lost in. There are so many expectations in life, from various sources: societal, cultural, familial, those set upon us by friends, colleagues, strangers, and, perhaps most crucially, ourselves, and it is hard to navigate it all, and to truly feel like we belong.

You're Never Too Much is an anthology which I hope will help you explore your feelings, as well as realize and appreciate that everything you feel is valid, everything you feel has purpose, and speaks to who you are as a person. There is no right or wrong way to be, only feelings which we can hone or lose ourselves in. Whether you're going through a heartbreak, a low period in your life, a moment of anxiety or depression, or simply feeling like the world is too much or crumbling around you, I hope you find words in this book that speak to our shared experiences at the moment you need to hear them.

Let's be proud, let's be bold, let's be forgiving, and let's be thankful for the way we've felt and the way we feel. Think of this anthology as a balm – not an antidote, but a soothing salve for every emotional wound, with words of wisdom from those who live in the same world we do. Trust me, you're not alone in the way you feel.

So feel it.

Charlie Castelletti, April 2025

Why

In the gaps between
dreams and
storms and
lies
I

    write

In the hollows of
night and
smiles and
hope
I

    write

In the shadows of
words and
trees and
kisses
I

    write   so I don't feel things anymore

         so I feel *everything*

            Attie Lime

Raw thoughts on 'too much'

Am I too much? Do I do too much? Laugh too much? Think too
much? Care too much? Ruminate on
the past too much? Make more of things too much? Cry too
much? Do nothing too much? Hurry too
much? Sleep too much? Stay awake too much? Eat too much?
Lay too much? Do I exist too much?
Want too much? Yearn too much? Ask too much? Withdraw too
much? Isolate too much? Talk too
much? Keep to myself too much? Edit too much? Critique too
much? Watch too much? See too
much? Hear too much? Taste too much? Feel? Too? Much? Am I
human too much? Too much, too
much? Too. Much. Too much? Too much no longer feels real at
this point of the paper. I wrote too
much, too much and it no longer feels real. I wonder if I do this to
myself too much, will I one day
disappear,
dissipate,
no longer real to the brain,
to the world?
Just like too much on the page, just like too much.

Christina Alejandra

I'M FEELING . . .
IN LOVE

Waffle House Crush

I'll have you smothered n covered n
diced n peppered n
capped n lathered n
lustred n smoothed n
spread

drizzled n dazzled n
blazed n baked n
blended n buttered n
shined n sprinkled n
seared

creamed n candied n
steamed n whipped n
stuffed n sugared n
spiced n simmered n
oiled,

reduced,

heaped,

dressed,

n can I get some coffee with that?

Harry Josephine Giles

O, Were I Loved As I Desire to Be!

O, were I loved as I desire to be!
What is there in the great sphere of the earth,
Or range of evil between death and birth,
That I should fear, – if I were loved by thee!
All the inner, all the outer world of pain,
Clear love would pierce and cleave, if thou wert mine;
As I have heard that somewhere in the main
Fresh-water springs come up through bitter brine.
'I were joy, not fear, clasped hand in hand with thee,
To wait for death – mute – careless of all ills,
Apart upon a mountain, though the surge
Of some new deluge from a thousand hills
Flung leagues of roaring foam into the gorge
Below us, as far on as eye could see.

Alfred, Lord Tennyson

enemies to lovers trope

i don't want to admit it
out loud, this infatuation with a
wound. the line where the threads
of my skin split, the ragged
breath where i
realize i am hurt
and don't feel it yet.

correction: i don't want to admit it
out loud, the enchantment of an
insult. the justice of it. the honesty.
the end of a long wait.
i can finally sleep, now.
i have never
been better loved than by
an enemy.

correction: i don't want to admit it
out loud, this regressive
longing. the way i want to lick your
shadow off the ground.
i know better, of course.
but i am by spellbound by insult.
i twitch at the smell of blood.
feral, maddened,
reverent.

Kelsey Day

Two Boys in the Dark

Your heart, a wild and untamed thing,
finally unleashed on the world.
Held in captivity, locked away behind layers of fear,
	finally free.

Falling for a sweet boy,
with soft eyes and an open face.
It had been a small thing,
a gesture that went unnoticed.

A compliment given,
fire kissing your cheeks,
unprepared for this. He was bold and beautiful, brazen
	with his words,
words like poetry to your ears.

A snowball that becomes an avalanche,
from kind words to gentle kisses.
His bedroom. The door bolted, the backs of your knees
	against the bed,
his hands holding you in place.
The world is asleep, but this room is alive.

Kisses that are fast, that are slow,
and a hunger that is insatiable.
Words spoken under heavy breath fill the room
    with electricity.
It sizzles and pops, illuminating this darkened room.

Your name falling from his lips,
placing soft kisses against your neck.
Hands searching,
tracing the outline of your body.

He listens as you open yourself,
your history and your heart falling into his hands.
A burden that is gifted,
shared between two boys in the dark.

Charlie Brodie

The perfect caress has a velocity of three centimetres per second

I read on the science of touch, a paper titled
Human C-Tactile Afferents are Tuned
to the Temperature of a Skin-Stroking Caress:
or, my need to have another body pressed to mine
      is built into me
like hunger or thirst.

Neurons wait for fingertips to trickle down my skin
like raindrops down a car window.

Bodies lose their mystery when you first kiss
      first cut corpses
            first feel your own fail (you).
Wonder is as relative as a race between
a hammer and a feather (a feather and a hammer)
and I never feel as eyebright as I did
when curiosity took me to dissection rooms
and the backrows of cinemas
      exploring bodies with light or without
      hands moving with hesitation.

Tonight my limbs encompass you
with the gentleness of a golden retriever
holding an egg in its mouth.

                          Jack Cooper

I Wish in the City of Your Heart

I wish in the city of your heart
you would let me be the street
where you walk when you are most
yourself. I imagine the houses:
It has been rainging, but the rain
is done and the children kept home
have begun opening their doors.

Robley Wilson

By-Product

I am the aftermath of the stars;
lovers will tell you that you are made of
stardust. Lovers will call you
a miracle. Lovers will remind you of
the slim and slipping odds that you should ever
have landed on this spinning rock, not least
at the same time that they did; lovers will teach you
to see your shape with kinder eyes.
Trust them. Even when they are liars.
Even when they are fleeting, no more stable or
familiar to you than those distant (and long dead) stars,
just trust them. Just for long enough to love
yourself hard and harshly. You will meet your best
and most loyal lover there in your bedroom.
There, in your mirror.

Aaron Cawood

I loved you first: but afterwards your love

I loved you first: but afterwards your love
Outsoaring mine, sang such a loftier song
As drowned the friendly cooings of my dove.
Which owes the other most? my love was long,
And yours one moment seemed to wax more strong;
I loved and guessed at you, you construed me
And loved me for what might or might not be –
Nay, weights and measures do us both a wrong.
For verily love knows not 'mine' or 'thine;'
With separate 'I' and 'thou' free love has done,
For one is both and both are one in love:
Rich love knows nought of 'thine that is not mine;'
Both have the strength and both the length thereof,
Both of us, of the love which makes us one.

Christina Rossetti

Valentine

Not a red rose or a satin heart.

I give you an onion.
It is a moon wrapped in brown paper.
It promises light
like the careful undressing of love.

Here.
It will blind you with tears
like a lover.
It will make your reflection
a wobbling photo of grief.

I am trying to be truthful.

Not a cute card or a kissogram.

I give you an onion.
Its fierce kiss will stay on your lips,
possessive and faithful
as we are,
for as long as we are.

Take it.
Its platinum loops shrink to a wedding ring,
if you like.
Lethal.
Its scent will cling to your fingers,
cling to your knife.

Carol Ann Duffy

Text

I tend the mobile now
like an injured bird

We text, text, text
our significant words.

I re-read your first,
your second, your third,

look for your small *xx*,
feeling absurd.

The codes we send
arrive with a broken chord.

I try to picture your hands,
their image is blurred.

Nothing my thumbs press
will ever be heard.

Carol Ann Duffy

I'M FEELING . . .
ANGRY

Red

He sees red everywhere.
Today, it's in the rain-hinting clouds
of the wind-chilled sky
and in the barista's overly enquiring eyes.
His coffee is crimson, his toasted sandwich scarlet.
Blazing now, his language flares
and he paints me with all the reds he has –
I'm puce, I'm flame, I'm folly.
Candy, carmine, coral.
Ruby, russet, fuchsia.
I'm cherry, I'm chilli, I'm brick,
I'm shocking pink.
Now, his red runs through my veins
and since my skin is thin,
it risks a spill.
The barista clears our cups.
A voice inside me rusts
and erupts: *Shit, man,*
can't you see I wasn't finished!

Shauna Darling Robertson

Betrayal

Rose, for the blooms that drew me in.
Ruby, for the ring that bought my fate.
Scarlet, for her nails, her lips, her sin.
Flame, for the grief that blazed to hate.
Brick, for the scars, my souvenirs.
Blood, for a heart that's been slashed in two.
Crimson, for eyes that are wrung with tears.
I see only red when I think of you.

Claire Schlinkert

This Be The Verse

They fuck you up, your mum and dad.
  They may not mean to, but they do.
They fill you with the faults they had
  And add some extra, just for you.

But they were fucked up in their turn
  By fools in old-style hats and coats,
Who half the time were soppy-stern
  And half at one another's throats.

Man hands on misery to man.
  It deepens like a coastal shelf.
Get out as early as you can,
  And don't have any kids yourself.

Philip Larkin

Charcuterie

Square teeth gummed
with grey filament,
cuspid and bicuspid,
cleave open my clavicle &
peck out the heart like a wet pip
sizzling. A glut, a guttering, head
engorged and swelling like a tick. *Santé.*

It is our own fault, really.
Diligent hands decode our bodies
to a riddle of bone, leave us segmented
in painless pieces.

Can you stomach me
now? Stripped and stippled
with shotgun pellets, a redblack
razzle-dazzle. I once heard
the tale of a hunter crucified
on a roe stag's antlers and now
that stag watches from the wall,
its grinning vice of empty jaws
complicit as a mother.
Entrecôte, anyone?

I understand now, why the pigs
came to eat their endings
from the palms of your hands,
how you made us into something
red, something to be washed
down with sauvignon.
Auberge espagnole of a rib-eyed
daughter, take what you please, don't
be shy. The unplugged heart spits
& shivers, vomiting runnels
of white fat on the plancha.

They always ask for it *saignant*.

Annabelle Cormack

Enough

A voice bursts through, whispering for destruction,
a renewal of self with a cry that burns eyes black

but tears won't incinerate this time: no feathers
conjured from ashes – instead, tears roll to form

an ocean, undulating like a dragon's serpentine back,
about to split open by a roar from your depths.

David Ly

When I argue, I forget to be me(ek)

I'm king and queen of this court. I'm jester
and knave, or parrot and linnet. I'm eagle
and dove, picking words like sticks
for the nest. I'm soaring high for effect,

beaking for laughs, swooping for emphasis,
dipping for grace. Shameless sweetness
exchanged for clear points outlined in pencil
sharp enough to peck out your eye. I tell you

you have made a category error. Glitter shakes
from my wings. I highlight inconsistencies.
It's galactic. I use words like *tergiversate*
and *mendacity*. *Eristic* and *stentorian*.

I can see the win like prey from the sky.
So what if I draw hearts. So what if I love you.

Deborah Finding

For When You Need Validation For Your Anger

You are angry and anxious
because you never agreed
to live in a burning home
while the people who should care
pretend the fire doesn't exist.

Distress
is a valid emotional response
to injustice.

Nikita Gill

A Poison Tree

I was angry with my friend:
I told my wrath, my wrath did end.
I was angry with my foe:
I told it not, my wrath did grow.

And I water'd it in fears,
Night & morning with my tears;
And I sunned it with smiles,
And with soft deceitful wiles.

And it grew both day and night,
Till it bore an apple bright;
And my foe beheld it shine,
And he knew that it was mine,

And into my garden stole
When the night had veil'd the pole:
In the morning glad I see
My foe outstretch'd beneath the tree.

William Blake

from Poem about My Rights

Even tonight and I need to take a walk and clear
my head about this poem about why I can't
go out without changing my clothes my shoes
my body posture my gender identity my age
my status as a woman alone in the evening/
alone on the streets/alone not being the point/
the point being that I can't do what I want
to do with my own body because I am the wrong
sex the wrong age the wrong skin and
suppose it was not here in the city but down on the beach/
or far into the woods and I wanted to go
there by myself thinking about God/or thinking
about children or thinking about the world/all of it
disclosed by the stars and the silence:
I could not go and I could not think and I could not
stay there
alone
as I need to be
alone because I can't do what I want to do with my own
body and
who in the hell set things up
like this

June Jordan

Happy New Year

Let's be arsonists. Let's burn the year.
Let's baptise each month in petrol and take a match
to day one. It was too good. Let's make like artists
and burn the libraries because we shouldn't and burn
Parliament because we should. Let's build a pyre
of everything that's lovely and everything that isn't
and burn it. Oh it will be glorious. The kittens will burn.
The christmas trees will burn. The traffic will burn.
The honeybees will burn. The oceans will burn. Oh the fires
will bloom like bruises on the Earth, which will burn,
and the sun will burn and the planets of gas will burn
and the planets of ice will burn and when the universe
has caught and needs no more tenderness from us
we will burn ourselves and the idea of fire.

Harry Josephine Giles

Too Angry

I am too angry at the world
To share a poem right now.

So go ahead and tear this page out.
Or scribble your thoughts if you prefer –
I've left the next pages blank for you.
But make sure to leave a dent or two.

Release your anger.
Leave your mark.

Feels good, right?
At least you got it all out.

Charlie Castelletti

Express your emotions here

I'M FEELING . . .
HEART/BROKEN

little recipe

Take my heart; mush it up until you get a thick paste. Don't worry if it hardens, it'll ease later. Keep whisking until stiff peaks form, that rise and jut. Now take the rest of the ingredients and gently fold them into the heart, making sure not to over beat. Each ingredient needs to be distinguishable, separated like a German *trennbares Verb*. In no condition do we want the heart assimilated, its taste floating softly above other flavours, like orange blossom, jasmine or Damascus rose in macaroons. Once you have the mixture, leave it for a few minutes to cool. You should see a slight change in texture and a deflation that is normal. Now turn it upside down, throw it on the floor and jump on it. Keep stamping vigorously until the mixture is completely flattened. Sprinkle a little bit of sugar then twist your feet, sliding from one side of the kitchen to the other. This will make sure that the heart is firmly in all the nooks and crannies and unable to be retrieved. Once you have done this, step back and admire, your mushed heart is now ready to enjoy.

Dide

If I can stop one Heart from breaking

If I can stop one Heart from breaking
I shall not live in vain
If I can ease one Life the Aching
Or cool one Pain

Or help one fainting Robin
Unto his Nest again
I shall not live in Vain.

Emily Dickinson

One Minute with Lavender

I drink green tea by my seedlings –
full of contagious desire to climb,
all of them –
can you see it?
I notice everything –
wayward feathers by my toes
the preferred flowers the bees go to.
Don't you know,
silver is one minute with lavender
when you love yourself,
gold the warming of your thighs under the sun?

I remember sitting with my broken heart
in Hyde Park in the heat,
not even seeing the grass I cried on.
Did birds sing? I ignored the tiny wings in fairy hues –
I only grew the single question of why –
lost seconds, weeks of shadow leaves
unfurling into my mind,
a rustling shade.

There is some kind of garden around you,
near you.
Know yourself, barefoot,
what you and the bumblebees like to drink,
glint so much the magpie flies down
for a minute.

LJ Ireton

Wreckages

The ocean floor is where the darkest, coldest things go to
live; extremophiles. The sort that can breathe in sulphur and
chew up rust and those are the creatures that might call a wreckage
beautiful. Fruitful garden, wrought-iron to keep out the
land-dwellers and things with souls, the sort that don't know
the difference between a death and an opportunity. Every wreckage
is a death to the living. The ocean floor is where the darkest,
coldest things go to peel off their skin clean, washed slick in
salt, cauterize the sinew where they had been coming apart at the
seams anyway. The closer you get, the uglier. Dearest
diver, leave the bones of me for the faceless bacteria and the almost-
maggots. Do not bother swimming close enough to touch
the white-hot line along my metal where an iceberg once plunged
daggers hard into my abdomen and just kept dragging
the wound open, and open, and open.

Aaron Cawood

Almost Feelings

Sometimes
you are going to miss a person
who was an almost to you.

And feel sad because
there is no name
for that feeling.

You just feel it in a way
that makes you tired
to your very bones.

Nikita Gill

Little Heartbreak

A little Heartbreak, wan and sore,
was sitting by herself. A sunbeam
slipped around the door and danced upon
a shelf. Though little Heartbreak knew
not why, she ceased, quite suddenly, to
cry. Still little Heartbreak sat alone.
'I never will be whole again,' thus said
she in her saddest tone, 'I never will be
healed of pain.' Then, unannounced, a
little breeze that had been playing in the
trees, passed softly over Heartbreak's
face, and, lo! of tears there was no trace.
Then when a bird began to sing, and
Heartbreak couldn't help but hear, there
happened such a curious thing – a silvern
echo did appear, enthroned itself in
Heartbreak's breast and, like the bird,
sang with sweet zest! So little Heartbreak
tossed her head and laughed to
find the world so fair. 'It's true,' she
cried, 'my heart has bled, and I have
lived with black despair. But I can't
be quite broken, long – with sunbeams,
zephyrs, and birds' song!'

Wilhelmina Stitch

What I've Learned From Heartbreak

That I matter. That my emotions, alive, are telling me to survive. That a heart that breaks into a million pieces is a heart that can spread through my whole body, and live in all of me. That there is a truth in tears, and a boldness in the bravery to cry. To say: *I feel.* I feel laughter and joy and happiness and fear and hurt and pain and that emotion with no name, the one that wrenches in my gut and drags at my lungs. And just when I think I don't know how to see my way through, I've learned that I can. That I will. That I *do.* I can become more myself in the more of me that I know, and every heartbreak is a chance to meet myself and grow. It's a chance to hold my own hand, which will make me stronger than any weightlifting can. There are no medals for this. This moment of battling through what you never wanted to. But there is me, and there is you. *You* are not alone. Even in the silence, there is the sound of a turn of a page. There is this poem, and the one you may write one day. There is your wisdom, the one that I know you hear. You can tell of it now, in this space. Right here.

Nadine Aisha Jassat

After

After your heart
breaks,

you'll study the pieces,
like a mug you loved
until it cracked.

You'll turn the shards over and over,
strain to see where the crack started,
        why it deepened,
the moment you could have stopped it,
        the moment it was too late.

None of this will change the mug's fate
but maybe

you'll refuse
to let sharp things cut you down.

You'll save the sad crumbs
for that mosaic you meant to make

and settle more gently
what's left on the shelf

until

one day

in the blank where your best mug belongs

you'll see a neat stack of new tomorrows
and brew the tea strong

because once
something inside you

broke

but now

there is
an after.

Tracie Renee

Heartbreak Echoes

There is, of course, that first momentous rip –
clear and fibrous and sharp
and so unlike any other pain you have ever felt.
Don't worry. It will heal.

It is the echoes that will get you,
dull and muffled that they are –
three months after bounding around that cavity in your chest,
hitting you as you stand in the grocery store checkout
and swear to God that's him the next queue over,
just a little bit shorter than you remember, and with greasier hair;
six months after, when you tell yourself you're ready
to go out on a date and you spend the night laughing and smiling and
you lean in for that first kiss and smell a familiar cologne
and never call him again;
two years after, when you are finally at peace
and you hear through mutual friends that
he's engaged, and she's pregnant, and
you're fine – *no, no* – you're fine.

Tim Stobierski

Let it let you let them go

let it ache, let it hurt, let it sting, let it rage, let it start, let it be, let
it exist, let it drop, let it twist and knot, let it play your ribcage like
windchimes, let it put your heart in your throat, let it sob, let it bite
and snarl and gnash its teeth, let it watch, let it wait, let it breathe,
let it hold you, let it see you, let it bask in this healing, let it be slow
and soft, let it be kind, let it understand, let it know you that you'll
never betray yourself again, let it give you the courage to walk
away, let it let you become strangers, let it romanticize life, let it
repair the things in you that you didn't break, let it love you and

– let it let you let them go

Pan Saville

I'M FEELING . . .

OVERWHELMED, ANXIOUS, OR LIKE I'M TOO MUCH

Grasping

There is no word
for nights that reach backwards
and help themselves to half the afternoon

or for a sea so starved,
it eats its own waves.

No word for the pebbles you turn
over and over in your hand,

weighing the waves against the world,
the night against the mind

and the weight of the mind
against its grasping for answers.

Shauna Darling Robertson

Knot

I've got a knot in my stomach.
That's what someone told me
when I tried to describe
how I was feeling
before a date.

But then I looked up knots
and it turns out
there are loads of them
and I think I've had them all at some point.

I had the clove hitch
which is a *versatile attaching hitch*
when I was trying to get myself
out of a bad relationship
and into a good one.

I had the overhead knot
which is a *basic stopper knot*
when I was just trying
to shut it all out.

I had the square knot
which is a *load-bearing knot*
when I was trying to take
some family pressure off my sister.

There's so many of these
I'm tying myself in knots.

Rob Walton

The Anxiety List

Finding exits in cramped rooms.

Drinking until rooms spin so I can speak.

Not being able to find a space for my voice, then taking up
   too much room.

Wearing two pairs of tights.

Checking seats after sitting down for blood or sweat.

Sweating through jumpers.

Rolling sleeves over knuckles, curling fingers into threads.

Not sleeping.

Waiting for people to come home.

Never wanting to open presents because it feels like jumping
   off a cliff.

Putting smiles on my face that I can't feel.

Looking forward to seeing people too much.

Cancelling plans.

Brushing my teeth twice.

Three times.

Holding my breath until I can't see.

Breathing so much I am dizzy.

Not eating.

Eating too much.

Changing my laugh.

Being scared of strangers in the street.

Thinking there are ghosts on the stairs.

Thinking people are looking at me.

Always looking at me.
Dreading tomorrow.
Dreading next week.
Dreading next month.
Next year.

Dread.

Lois Foster

The Healing List

Finding entrances with friends.
Knowing I am good enough on my own.
Breaking silence because I can.
Wearing what I want.
Not checking what's on the seat because I don't have to;
    everybody sweats and that is life.
Sweating because it's normal (but there are treatments for
    hyperhidrosis; I should know!).
Having my hands out in all their clammy glory.
Sleeping because anxiety doesn't keep me up anymore; if it does,
    then I know it won't last forever.
Remembering that most of the time, people come back.
Accepting that opening presents are part of life and love.
Wearing a smile I feel inside.
Knowing that anxiety and excitement are close friends.
Doing plans (but it's okay to cancel sometimes: healing isn't linear).
Brushing my teeth and stopping when they're clean.
Taking deep breaths.
Eating with the people around me.
Laughing with no inhibitions.

Opening doors for people and smiling.

Making friends with the ghosts on the stairs.

If people look at me, let them look.

Letting tomorrow,

next week,

next month,

next year come.

Live.

Lois Foster

I WANT ! TO WANT ! TO LIVE !

after Chrissy Williams

I want ! to want ! to live ! I want
to go outside ! & give witness !
to sunset ! or to shadows !
what blanket the dust-colored hills !
I want ! to call them golden ! not dry !
not dead ! not another reminder !
of how rarely it rains ! O I want
to be freed ! of this nagging need !
the endless search ! for something !
to tether me ! to this earth ! &
I am too old ! to be this unwell !
but look ! here I am ! writing
another poem about nightfall !
which is maybe a metaphor ! O
the day is done ! only darkness now !
only a girl-body lying in the field !
which is really her bed ! O her
crumpled sheets ! O & outside !
an owlsound marks the dusk !

Despy Boutris

Natural Buoyancy

I take the plunge,
this time I'm deadly serious,
with my sack of angst
I'm heading for the depths.

But hardly am I under
than I'm beginning to see the funny side.
Why is there always a funny side?
And before I know it,

all weightiness jettisoned,
I'm back to floundering
foolishly on the surface.
It's such a curse this natural buoyancy.

Philip Waddell

Jack-in-the-Box

autism spectrum disorder, at age 20

I am a gorilla   but caged
with flamingos and macaws
  such colour!   I cover
my eyes   with leaves

in the mulch   I become small
  between wall   and tree trunk
woodlice walk   over my ankles

I am learning   not to make a fuss
  putting my hands in my mouth
      so screams press
against them   a Jack-in-the-Box
drumming his head against his wooden lid

too old to be afraid
  of supermarkets   where tomatoes
pulse with fluorescence

or of the vacuum cleaner's roar
   shattering my   skull and teeth
like eggshell

by the front door
   a harvest-man   translates
his jumble of legs and wings
   into a French-lace shadow

my only ally
   like me   he waits
for   a parenthesis
   (   )

Rosamund Taylor

Portrait of My Anxiety as an Imp

My imp comes with me everywhere I go.
She tugs my hair and curls her silky tail
so tight around my neck she stops airflow;
when she's nervous she chews my nails
until they bleed. She's afraid on busy streets,
in classrooms and in pubs. She clawed free
at the concert hall: she nipped people's feet
and howled as violins and cellos rose in key.

Long ago, she survived in woods and fenland,
she hid from falcons and relentless bears,
sleeping in pine-needles, shivering downwind.
But now she's safe indoors. Foxes are scared,
eagles poisoned: she still won't believe she's fine,
there are no jaws waiting to snap her spine.

Rosamund Taylor

Trans Anxiety

Anxiety as a trans person feels heightened.
I can feel the ripples of wind stick to me as I walk,
churning around – around the aether of my being,
roaring, screaming into discombobulated thoughts
and fears of rejection. Every gaze in my direction is
its own separate sun scorching through the protective
layers of my irises, burning all my gender-affirming clothes
into piles of ashes upon my toes, melting all the make-up
from the dark shadows to my nose. I constantly feel
like I am on the edge, like a carpet beneath my feet is
slowly being pulled by an outside force and I have no way
of knowing when or if the pulling will stop. There are rare
moments where I find a place of calm, control, collectiveness
and it's usually when the weather is nice, when I feel like I am
in good company and can map out how the next few minutes,
hours are going to turn out. When I know that whatever happens
next that I am not alone. There is always people to turn to,
a home to come back to, a place to escape from the world
when I need to rest and focus on my own health.

Aidan Summers

Hypocrite

I'm a hypocrite sometimes.
I shame myself for feeling ashamed of myself,
Positively obsessive about body positivity
I weep when my own jeans are too tight.
I tell my friends not to be a doormat,
Demand that they demand,
While I'm head-to-toe in size 10 footprints.
The remains of every person I couldn't say no to,
I offer other sage financial advice,
Ignoring the overdraft letter that lives under my bed,
Waiting, like a debt-ridden monster,
To pounce when I finally rest.
I wonder if I'm a narcissist,
As I scroll through endless photos of myself,
Critiquing each pixel as I pass,
Before commenting that we all just need to let go,
It's freeing not to care,
As if I don't, as if I'm so laid back that none of these things matter.
Because they don't.
I'm a hypocrite sometimes.

Charlotte Moore

Wildfires burn across Australia as Edward Cullen takes his shirt off for the twentieth time

A thousand miles

away a country burns

as we decide it is time

for a Twilight

marathon

silvery moon

cold skin

in my heart

as Bella moves from Phoenix,

Arizona

making me see climate refugees

even in my YA

we cannot see the flames

like bees we are

asleep

smoked out

impervious

to our home

dissolving

Jacob says

to Edward

'I'm hotter than you'

which is true

but not all things that are true
are heard
new moon
breaking dawn
light still crawling
but as the sun cracks its yolk on
our popcorn husks
the dead
weight
in my stomach
is undying
I am cored
an apple
wishing
its pips will still be
seeded
find ground in which
to live
that the venomous bite
of rubbish
of sewage
of the crushed snail
of the dead wasp on the pavement
is not eternal
that the sharp pains in my chest will be
eclipsed
by action

(my own included)
and that it was okay
– forgive me –
to watch Bella and Edward
get their happy ending
whilst a country burned.

Elspeth Wilson

Poetry Submission

Dear poetry editor,
When you read my submission of three poems
think of me dumping a heavy metal box labelled
– *TRAUMA* –
in front of your crammed desk with a bang,
and when you suspiciously open the box,
think of unpacking the dusty creepy skeleton model
your science teacher used to explain human bone structure
and skeletal abnormalities while nobody listened,
as paper planes soared in the air high on suppressed laughter.
Think of pulling out the creased letter enclosed in the rib cage,
unfolding the sheet and discovering a clumsy blob of ink –
that was me pouring my pain on the page,
for you to consider if it's legible enough,
if I've crawled deep enough into the darkness,
and dragged out just enough dirt to intrigue you,
but not quite as much as to put you off in disgust,
as I need you to take part of my ballast hostage
for a while, jailed in the pages of your magazine.

In a nutshell, dear poetry editor,
I submit my anxiety to your forthcoming issue.
Yet, for now, I refuse to submit to my anxiety issues.

Christina Hennemann

Overshare

Open up, you say
and I prolapse in a stutter of ragged morse
as you chop the celery.

Here is
a duck's severed head in a drinking glass,
and trains, what ridiculous things,
pulling in and out like lovemaking,
all those little people
hurrying for shelter or taxis or bagels,
all taking themselves utterly seriously and

At supper do you see a wreath of eyes
blinking in the churn of your rabbit stew?
And suppose
you woke up and found your face replaced
with a roulette wheel spinning into nothingness
what then?

Here are the things I have done and they are
mostly bad. Separate into component elements,
easier to ingest. Words beginning with v:
velveteen, vociferous, viagra.
I give you them in my other language,
the one that means something,
and here is the sound of your knife
on the block sharpening.

O tender, o tenderloin.
The pot is boiling over, you say,
also you are leaving a stain. Hush,
hush, the bedroom is down the hall.

When you asked me to open up

you did not mean like that.

Annabelle Cormack

Anxiety

if stands for
irreversible future
stands for
I should have thought of that
I better think of it
I better stop it

what if
what if
    were not
    a curse

what if
what if
    could be
    a game
    of how far
    we can dream

but what if
making
what if
a game
lifts so much weight
off our shoulders

we lose touch
with gravity

what if we float away
what if we can't stay
in the dream
what if we reverse
the good future
what if we irreverse
the tired now

what if
we pack every misfortune
into a suitcase
hand it to what if and send them
ahead in time
where *if* so longs to go
we wave them goodbye and
    return
    to the present
    to breathing
    in the steady rhythm of now

what then?

Casper E. Falls

You're Never Too . . .

You're never too poor to give away kindness,
you're never too rich to feel sadness or fear,
you're never too quiet to make others listen,
you're never too loud to stop and to hear.

You're never too guilty to ask for forgiveness,
you're never too flawless to need help to cope,
you're never too big to feel ever-so-tiny,
you're never too little to give someone hope.

You're never too foolish to try to be wiser,
you're never too wise to need time to heal,
you're never too this or too that to make changes,
you're never too young to say how you feel.

Laura Mucha

I'M FEELING . . .
HOPEFUL

Small Green Thing

I'm going to be a leaf today.
I shall fall all over the place
in decorative fashion, the wind posting me
haphazardly through slots in the air.
So much will be possible in my covert laboratory.
I shall invent outlandish rituals,
new ways of being flat and important.
I shall write *Diary of a Modern Leaf*,
describing my thrashing about in vibrant prose.
I shall swoop and ascend, startled
by my own patterns, how I keep pointing
like a signpost toward delight
which, lost so long, turned up again,
stupid, beautiful and forgiven, like the sun.

John McCullough

Hope

Oh, I forgot to tell you!
Hope re-entered the room.
Remember her from all those years ago?
Remember how she'd sashay through doorways
and spring through open windows,
lift you up by the waist,
carry you around,
and you'd wrap your arms around her sturdy shoulders,
tasting sweet, warm swallows of sunshine,
while the world blasted all its delicious colors at you
like an old Technicolor movie?
Remember how your heartbeat would awaken
and rattle out a little tap dance in your chest –
tap-tappity-tap-tap!
And a fiery flame flared to life inside you,
sometimes burning for days.
Or even weeks.
Even months!
You could do absolutely *anything*.
Until we lost our Hope.

We didn't even realize she'd left, did we?
They tossed her into a gaping hole in the ground
and shoveled rocks and rubble over her bare, bleeding back,
and we withered without her.
But remember how you used to sing for the sheer joy of singing,
instead of swimming through the murk and the muck of
the horrors haunting that cold little contraption you cradle in your
    hands?
We could have that again.
Oh, I forgot to tell you!
Hope reentered the room, out of the blue, on a summer
    afternoon.
And I wonder, why didn't we all grab shovels and dig her out much
    sooner?
What were we doing all those years?

Cat Winters

Glossary for Hope

	EXPECTATION	CHANGE	HOPE	JOY
MEANING	the future is a diffuse light, beaming in a straight line ahead of you	the path forward splinters open	the beautiful possibilities spilling out from disparate futures	all this hope has paid off
SYNONYMS	false certainty	toiling	watching	the life
ANTONYMS	the shadow	strict	forgetting	the misery
GREAT LOVES	clarity	the outer	recurrent	this time, this place, this moment

Munira Tabassum Ahmed

Good News

Good news waits
like a freshly planted sunflower seed,
a full moon during the day,
friends at a birthday party
ready to yell SURPRISE.

Good news arrives
like a milkman before breakfast,
snow on Christmas morning,
fresh bread in a toaster.

Good news hits
like strawberry ice cream
on a warm tongue,
a firework on a black sky,
a cat leaping on to a lap.

Carl Burkitt

Today is a good day

Something finally clicked over in my brain
– not that it had felt like some kind of meter,
like I was forever crawling my tired way nearer.
No: it was more gone than here, the something.
But then it *returned*, a silky wave of electrons,
a warm whirlpool of hormones into my blood,
like reflections rushing into being in the water.

Something huge or tiny had shifted in the sky,
and I will never understand what, nor need to.
I just know the clouds glowed, and they will again,
and the geese saw how peaceful their river was,
how hopeful, and they honked their approval,
stomped great feet, and the water felt even better
and it swirled with joy and relief, and then slept.

Elizabeth Gibson

Small Kindnesses

I've been thinking about the way, when you walk
down a crowded aisle, people pull in their legs
to let you by. Or how strangers still say 'bless you'
when someone sneezes, a leftover
from the Bubonic plague. 'Don't die,' we are saying.
And sometimes, when you spill lemons
from your grocery bag, someone else will help you
pick them up. Mostly, we don't want to harm each other.
We want to be handed our cup of coffee hot,
and to say thank you to the person handing it. To smile
at them and for them to smile back. For the waitress
to call us honey when she sets down the bowl of clam chowder,
and for the driver in the red pick-up truck to let us pass.
We have so little of each other, now. So far
from tribe and fire. Only these brief moments of exchange.
What if they are the true dwelling of the holy, these
fleeting temples we make together when we say, 'Here,
have my seat,' 'Go ahead – you first,' 'I like your hat.'

Danusha Laméris

"Hope" is the thing with feathers

"Hope" is the thing with feathers –
That perches in the soul –
And sings the tune without the words –
And never stops – at all –

And sweetest – in the Gale – is heard –
And sore must be the storm –
That could abash the little Bird
That kept so many warm –

I've heard it in the chillest land –
And on the strangest Sea –
Yet, never, in Extremity,
It asked a crumb – of Me.

Emily Dickinson

Because the World Didn't End

because the world didn't end when i came out as bisexual
because the world didn't end when i came out as trans
because the world didn't end when i asked for help
because the world didn't end when i went to therapy
because the world didn't end when i was assaulted
because the world didn't end when my friendships did
because the world didn't end when i was fired
because the world didn't end when i tried to die

because the world became so much fuller when i recognized my
    trauma
because the world became so much fuller when i kissed a girl
because the world became so much fuller when i kissed a boi
because the world became so much fuller when i discovered T4T
    love

because the world became so much fuller when i got on a plane
    and left,
and got on a plane and came back
because the world became so much fuller when i realized
not everything has happy endings
because the world became so much fuller when i found queer
    community
because the world became so much fuller when i found chosen
    family

and chosen family taught me how to fulfil love
and chosen family taught me how to heal and repair

because the world became so much fuller when i realize i can't fix it
my only responsibility i believe
is to hold on
as it spins.

Cal Brantley

The First Cosmonaut

Travel through life
as though life is the cosmos

as though you are the first person
to fly into its void .

as though your outstretched arms
are powered by the sun

as though your body
is the mathematics of freedom

as though your fingers
speak the only language there is

as though your eyes
are newborn stars in a nebula

as though your heart
can survive a supernova

as though each day
is a new planet

as though each year
is weightless

as though each moment
is an atom

as though solitude
is fuel

as though even if you land
you will always fly again

Dom Conlon

When You Ask Me If I Can Say Yes to the World as It Is

Today yes is made of lead.
You look at me
and I nod –
and together
we carry the weight.

Rosemerry Wahtola Trommer

Finish Lines

Marathons and races have pace-setters,
They set the rhythm of different speeds,
Marking sprints, runs, moderate jogs,
Having different goals but taking the lead.
Life is not a race, though, honey,
You get to set your very own tempo,
Maybe you sprint, maybe you crawl,
But you have to live in your own flow.
People might speed past, overtake you,
Make you feel slow or leave you behind,
But the people at your speed will find you,
And all of us make it to the finish line.
But our finish lines are different, love,
We all need and want different things,
And finding your own unique trail
Really is the only true way to win.
But what I'm really trying to say is:
There's no 'right' way to be yourself,
You're perfect just the way you are,
You don't need to be like anyone else.
The things you bring to the world, babe,
Are exactly what the world needs,
We need both bread and roses,
And you're the wheat and the seeds.

Life is not a race, sweet darling,
So live it however you want,
With the people who smile when you smile,
And not with the people who don't.
Don't let anyone make you feel less than,
Inferior or like you don't matter,
You're a treasure, a gift, a legend,
And you existing makes the world better.

Emma Hutson

If I Can't

If I can't walk that fast,
then I'll start a new race.
If I can't keep my balance,
then I'll sing as I sway.
If I can't use my hand,
then I'll learn a new trick.
If I get so very tired,
then I'll run in my sleep.
If the heat is too much,
then I'll wave at the sun.
If I forget the answer,
then I'll find a new question.
If I can't sleep at night,
then I'll say good morning to the stars.

Julie Stevens

This Too Will Pass

This, too, will pass. Oh, heart, say it over and over
Out of your deepest sorrow, out of your grief,
No hurt can last forever, perhaps tomorrow
Will bring relief.

This, too, will pass. It will spend itself, its fury
Will die as the wind dies down at the set of sun;
Assuaged and calm you will rest at last, forgetting
A thing that is done.

Repeat it again and again, oh, heart, for your comfort:
This, too, will pass, as surely as passed before
The old forgotten pain and the other sorrows
That once you bore.

As certain as stars at night or dawn after darkness,
Inherent as the lift of the blowing grass,
Whatever your despair or your frustration –
This, too, will pass.

Grace Noll Crowell

I Am Alone

I am alone.
Alone, like one dandelion weed launched upwards from the green.
I am alone,
Alone, like one jellyfish floating in the seaweed of the sea.
I am alone, like one person aside the railroad tracks.
I am alone,
Alone, like one popping corn who never ever cracks.
I'm alone,
Alone, like one bubble who floats a bit further afield than the rest.
I am alone,
Alone, like the solitary mountain who peaks into a sharp crest.

I am alone . . .

I am alone like one star in the beautiful, black sky, neighboured by
other lone stars, surrounded by shafts of space and luminous
   white . . .
There are so many of us up here –
Alone and illuminating . . .
Glowing and clarifying the wondrous infinite sky!

Perhaps I am not so alone.
Maybe I am a miniature, magical piece of a galaxy.

Carmella de Keyser

I'M FEELING . . .
REMINISCENT

The Sunflower Sonnets

she tells me her favourite flowers are sunflowers
says her favourite colour is yellow   not that that is the reason
she loves sunflowers   she loves their purity
their distinctive responsiveness to each other   when
the sun cannot be found they turn to comfort one another
as if huddling against the bulldozing winter   the way
a mother will nurse her child to her bosom   or
the way friends linger that little bit
too long when they know that something isn't right   that
the numbers aren't quite adding up to happy
I wonder how many times she has been that sunflower   I wonder
how many times she has been a golden sponge for toxins
how many times she has allowed anyone to see
that liquid-yellow wholesomeness that blooms within her heart

each day I pass them   those sunflowers in the vases
of the restaurant opposite my flat   and each day I think
of you   I imagine you in a field of poised sunflowers   the sun
straddling your back   as if it is you it needs
to survive   and the sunflowers   each one of them
singing you choruses of praise   each one of them
gilded by your presence   each one of them
lurched at the edge of their tip-toeing roots   their rounded faces
stretching their hard-leather necks that they might snatch
a glimpse of you   like summer's blush

you are a vision of meditated patience   luminated effigy
strolling the unfurled labyrinth of nature's walkways
the soil warm beneath your tread   and you know
that each velvet spread leads you here   leads you home

Dale Booton

Me and G
#1 Grandpa

Me: Gran, where did you first meet Grandpa?

G: It was in a wee village called Luss on the banks of
    Loch Lomond. He was sitting on the jetty.

Me: What was he doing?

G: He was just sitting there.

Me: Doing what?

G: Just sitting.

Me: And then what happened?

G: I said, 'Do you mind if I sit here?'

Me: And what happened after that?

G: He nodded, so I sat beside him.

Me: And then what did you do?

G: We just sat there.

Me: You just sat there?

G: We just . . . sat there.

Me: And then what?

G: We looked at the loch. The sun was going down.
    It was very calm, so it was. So was he. So was I.
    Very calm, the pair of us. Very peaceful.

Me: What did you say to him?

G: Nothing.

Me: What did he say to you?

G: Nothing.

Me: Nothing?

G: Nothing. We didn't speak. Not a word.

Me: ? ? ?

G: I remember it like it was yesterday.

Stewart Ennis

Walking in the Arboretum at Night

A girl and her mother, holding hands, walk an intermittently lit path, surrounded by rows of dark trees. Each tree is dedicated to a person that no longer exists in the physical world.

The girl lets go of her mother's hand and sits on a bench. Her mother watches her for a while, standing in place. The girl closes her eyes.

Her mother sighs and keeps walking down the path, without her.

The girl says, 'You know, a memory is kinda like a chair. You build it, and then you sit in it, for a while.'

The girl opens her eyes. Her mother is still walking away. She stays on the bench, watching her mother get smaller and smaller.

Rainie Oet

Deep Dish

I'm suddenly taken aback
by a particular brand of
microwaveable pizza   which unearths
a clump of memories
from my chilhood

On Sundays   at his house
at the start of the century   specifically
his microwave would congeal
the cheese to glistening perfection

I realize that this
is a nice memory

                 That
in the years since   I hadn't
felt such a fondness   or contentment
or warmth from dwelling
on that period of my life at all

                                        But this
recollection was just as it was   just of
the senses   and of food

                              A child's
microwaved pizza   and a feeling
of enjoying it somewhere difficult

                        Peter Scalpello

A Thunderstorm in Town

(A Reminiscence: 1893*)*

She wore a new 'terra-cotta' dress,
And we stayed, because of the pelting storm,
Within the hansom's dry recess,
Though the horse had stopped; yea, motionless
    We sat on, snug and warm.

Then the downpour ceased, to my sharp sad pain,
And the glass that had screened our forms before
Flew up, and out she sprang to her door:
I should have kissed her if the rain
    Had lasted a minute more.

Thomas Hardy

'I Thought of You'

I thought of you and how you love this beauty,
    And walking up the long beach all alone
I heard the waves breaking in measured thunder
    As you and I once heard their monotone.

Around me were the echoing dunes, beyond me
    The cold and sparkling silver of the sea –
We two will pass through death and ages lengthen
    Before you hear that sound again with me.

Sara Teasdale

Blackberries

The summer Frank Ocean dropped Channel Orange
we sat on the third-floor balcony
of Grandma's house, and
ate purple blackberries
sat in a white colander
cool from the fridge, at midnight, staining our fingers
purple-and-black, staining walls and white linen
with our fingers until
our stomachs swelled.

The summer I picked my own blackberries I was twenty-two.
I was in West Sussex.
I was staining my soul black until the green leaves became purple,

thinking of my grandmother staining her sheets in despair and
how being an adult is picking blackberries
then freezing them in batches for next year's crumble,
an empty colander in a heaving fridge of cheeses and meats;
but all you remember is the summer Frank Ocean dropped
Channel Orange and The starshine always kept you warm
and you ate blackberries by the fistful under clear night skies
watching bats flying circles around street lamps,
children playing hide-and-seek.

Goosebumps when the temperature drops.
The hairs on each purple berry standing on end.

The August sun was hot and round and orange and your hands
    were purple and black and
bruised, Ocean on a loop, peeling oranges in the morning while
    you ate the purple
blackberries.

Dredhëza Maloku

Sometimes . . .

Sometimes when I stand
with my toes at the edge
of the doorway
I think I still see you.

Sometimes when I sit
on the bench where you first shared
your secrets with me
I think I still hear you.

Sometimes when I reach
up to where you softly
stroked my hair
I think I still feel you.

Sometimes when I play
the record we bought together
I think I still –

feel your arms round my waist
see that look changing in your eyes
hear the sharp edge of your words
feel your breath graze my cheek
feel our bodies sway and stagger and stumble

and then.

I remember.

You're
gone.

Sometimes . . .

I'm not sure   which   I prefer.

Emma Perry

Eulogy

we should have funerals for places

i want to weep for airing cupboards and alleyways
friend's houses and family pubs

i want to collectively mourn my primary school cloakroom
the smell of pencil shavings and orange juice

i want to write a eulogy for the corner shop
it used to sell christmas trees, now breakfast butties

i want to wail a hymn for the supermarket near the library
(once somerfield, now tesco)
how i hated trudging down those aisles
now only ghosts do it
and i'm one of them

i want to bake fudge for the local park
where my best friend broke my heart
a glass muscle, wasted on 2am tarmac
let me carry out a final, sombre ritual
at the tarnished, monkey-bar shrine
in honour of what we were

and never came to be
and everything we became instead

Emmy Clarke

Later

our salt and pepper cat
has taken to sleeping on my desk chair
i have taken to sitting by him
watching the slow rise and fall
of his barrelled chest
kissing his hamburger-shaped noggin and
laying my ear against his shaved tummy
to hear his elderly rumble

later
in the garden
my partner cups that soft old chin and
sniffs the breath between his fangs
savouring the stench
i wish it were possible to package up
his eau du poisson breath
keep it in my pocket and
save it for later

later
he won't be here
only his salt and pepper shape
on the fabric of my desk chair
embedded
never to be lint rolled

Emmy Clarke

It's only a number

I still call your mobile to hear your voice.
And for the briefest of moments you are still here.
The pause, the hesitation, that was you.
I hang up before the answer services comes on.
I don't want to lose you again.

Until the day someone else answers
and I realize your number has been recycled.
It's only a number and I tell them it doesn't matter.
But it does.

Jer Hayes

24 hour Tesco

it's too late to remember what I came to Tesco for
but I know it had something to do with the last time we spoke
in your room we were both in facemasks and I was thirsty
which made me tell you the truth for once admitting
that I needed a glass of water more than anything else
to carry on you found a glass you were protecting in a drawer
from COVID-19 and walked out of the door for the first time
leaving me alone in the room
like life beyond therapy where you'll leave the world before me
now in Tesco I walk towards the boxes of tissues and think about
whether you've ever had a client who has walked away
with your tissue box before or asked you where you bought
them from so they could have a souvenir with which to say goodbye

Jo Morris Dixon

you.again

I think I have to write this down
Because how else can I say it
I am not the first
To write about a kiss
But like so many
I believe i am the first
To feel like this.

Does that make it
any less
worthy?

it was the second time
we met and
seconds soon became minutes
then hours
that is always how the story goes.

and we wrote ours
Into oblivion.

You said I had the softest skin
but my heart it would seem
is still softer

you liked the way
I glowed.
Pale
White
Luminous

I liked the way
you spoke.
Quiet
Tender
Gently

I remember thinking about what I would feel
when it was over
tracing some kind of definition
into a moment that
I might not believe
was real

But was anything that night?

Our bodies tumbling
Over words
Our arms linked
Over one another
Your hands running
Over me.

It all
still lingers.

You hid behind a cap
I hid behind a smile.
The light was spectral then
But the feeling wasn't.

I'm still writing this story
the one where
you called me a ghost
because that was our thing.

but now I'm the one haunted
and you're only disappearing

Tom Flanagan

I'M FEELING . . .
JOYFUL

For the Guy Who Keeps Telling Me to Smile

You're telling me to smile. Why?
To show you I'm besotted?
All right. I'll flash my fangs and then –
I'll come for your carotid.

Lisa Varchol Perron

The Orange

At lunchtime I bought a huge orange –
The size of it made us all laugh.
I peeled it and shared it with Robert and Dave –
They got quarters and I had a half.

And that orange, it made me so happy,
As ordinary things often do
Just lately. The shopping. A walk in the park.
This is peace and contentment. It's new.

The rest of the day was quite easy.
I did all the jobs on my list
And enjoyed them and had some time over.
I love you. I'm glad I exist.

Wendy Cope

Shining Things

I love all shining things – the lovely moon,
The silver stars at night, gold sun at noon.

A glowing rainbow in a stormy sky,
Or bright clouds hurrying when wind goes by.

I love the glow-worm's elf-light in the lane,
And leaves a-shine with glistening drops of rain,

The glinting wings of bees, and butterflies,
My purring pussy's green and shining eyes.

I love the street-lamps shining through the gloom,
Tall candles lighted in a shadowy room,

New-tumbled chestnuts from the chestnut tree,
And gleaming fairy bubbles blown by me.

I love the shining buttons on my coat,
I love the bright beads round my mother's throat.

I love the coppery flames of red and gold,
That cheer and comfort me, when I'm a-cold.

The beauty of all shining things is yours and mine,
It was a lovely thought of God to make things shine.

Elizabeth Gould

I Am Carrying Happiness

I am happy
it's so simple

I am carrying happiness
in my hands
I scarcely dare breathe
I'm afraid
of dropping it
as though I had to cross a desert
carrying a bowl of water
as though I'd picked up
a baby for the first time

I'm afraid
if I hold it too tight
it might break
and if I hold it too loosely
it could slip through my fingers

suffering wasn't like this
it was much more familiar
I knew where I stood with it
now my feet barely touch
the ground

now I don't know
how to behave at all
I am carrying happiness
in my hands

Maria Jastrzębska

Happiness, as a Dress

I am trying on happiness
like a new dress from a posh boutique –
a luxury I can't afford to pay for.
I'm worried that I've smuggled it out
and someone will hunt me down
and demand I give it back.
But I'll say I've only borrowed it,
taken it for a test run, like a new car
or any other expensive investment
that you have to be sure about
before you commit to the repayments.
It might not suit, after all.
My bum might look too big in it.
I might find that the neighbours stop
being kind to me if I'm in my happy dress.
They'll maybe start saying things like
You don't suit yellow.

I wonder what underwear I should be wearing?
If maybe I'll get a little cold
without a thermal vest or a thick cardigan?
Do I need posh shoes?
I'm not sure how to wash this type of dress.
Does happiness need to be dry-cleaned?
What happens if I'm caught in a sudden rain-shower?
Will this kind of material shrink, feel too tight?
Should I have it altered so it has a low-cut back?
Maybe take out some of the tucks in the waist
and add some elastic?

If I mess around with it too much will it
still be a happy dress? Or merely content?
Comfortable? Everyday wear?

Hannah Linden

The Best Medicine

This is me, laughing. And this one is my
brother and me on the boat, both laughing.
We're sending ripples out across the pond.
In this one we are trying not to laugh,
but laughing all the same. When my sister

joins us for this sequence in the garden,
she has got hiccups from laughing too much
and all three of us have tears in our eyes.
Even my father is shaking the camera,
pretending not to be amused at all.

There was the time in the minster – this is
the one – when someone came across to us
to ask us why we were laughing so much.
We hadn't stopped since we came in the door.
We are laughing, said my mother, because

(and here I pick up my father's camera
to capture, as they say, the occasion)
because, she says, our lives are amusing.
And she begins to laugh, her laughter as
infectious as any we've ever heard.

Even when fighting we couldn't help but
laugh at the pain we were inflicting or
suffering, laughable with its bruises
and tears. My brother laughed as he hit me
and I doubled up, laughing for dear breath.

Then what do you think we did when the dog,
with that usual laughing look on his face,
ran out into the road regardless of
the furniture van, squealing with its brakes?
What else could we have done – what else but laugh?

There must have been something in the water
for ten or fifteen years, something funny
in the water while we were growing up,
constantly triggering our reflexes,
leaving us helpless with mirth. Our shoulders

shook whenever silence was asked of us:
for one would always set the others off.
Our voices rang out in wave after wave,
feeding each other's laughter with laughter,
heartily laughing at nothing at all.

Gregory Woods

What a Joy It Is

Harry Woodgate

Don't Hesitate

If you suddenly and unexpectedly feel joy,
don't hesitate. Give in to it. There are plenty
of lives and whole towns destroyed or about
to be. We are not wise, and not very often
kind. And much can never be redeemed.
Still, life has some possibility left. Perhaps this
is its way of fighting back, that sometimes
something happens better than all the riches
or power in the world. It could be anything,
but very likely you notice it in the instant
when love begins. Anyway, that's often the
case. Anyway, whatever it is, don't be afraid
of its plenty. Joy is not made to be a crumb.

Mary Oliver

I'M FEELING . . .

FEARFUL, OR INSECURE

What Will Become of Me?

i'm scared of being nothing.
how stupid does that sound?
i'm scared of my life withering away to ash
scattered along the floorboards
collecting with the filth and grime in the corners of the room.
becoming an item on a shelf sprinkled in a jar
dust in the air the world breathes.
my memory held in a collectable photo album people will flip past
    for a second until they turn the page.
i'm scared all that will be left are these words on a screen
journals with cursed handwriting
caged feelings that weigh you down
forcing you to lock the book away before my spirit escapes.
i'm scared my goals will decay off my withering bones.
my dreams growing plot holes like moth-eaten clothes.
everything becoming unreachable like pretty stars that promise a
    brighter tomorrow
that never comes.
i'm scared this is all i'll be.
decayed down to poem after poem
trying to capture exactly what i mean
exactly how i feel
exactly what the meaning of myself is.

Raye Halabuza

Profile Picture Insecurity

You know, if you got to know me, I think you'd like me
You know, past the follower count and social likes, judgments of
    what I post of my small life
I'm still a person behind a screen, but so are you
Sever the electricity in our veins for something kinder, slower,
    mossier
Find me at the safe landing spot, the peace I want to earn and strive –
I'll be dressed in blue and showered in wisteria
Not a front, not an elusive ruse
Me (really, me?)
Yes, really me
I'm still here, and I think you'd like me

Sarah Peters

I Am Trying

This is what it looks like when
what is left by the vulture regrows its
legs and writhes, half-breathing, half-
bleeding, half-wretched and
swears that dying is just another way of
learning to walk and talk again. Foetus, foul
halfling, fucking freak show, top-billed
circus clown in make-up cracking over
sweat and cursing, yes, swearing that
even a carcass can find its feet.

Love is disgusting. To be so seen, so
unflinching, corpse reanimated just to be
touched and known and loved and, yes,
love *is* disgusting. The horror of living made
canon and carnal by the knowledge that you
are being watched as you go.

Aaron Cawood

Fear has me frozen

I am standing
at the edge
of the ice rink.

Clutching the gate
with numb fingers.
Frozen breath
gripping my lungs.

One step forward.

My first wobbling hop –
onto the gliding surface
of uncertainty.

My knees are liquid
Heart hammering hail

And falling is inevitable
Not if but when
The toe pick teeth
waiting to chew the ice
and spit me out.

With my first tumbling mistake.

But once I find my centre –
Gravity and hard won courage

Glide free
into possibility
and anxiety falls away.

Melting into the ice
with exhilaration.

I might still fall
The fear moves me forward
Doing it, anyway.

Charlie Morris

Mask

I've worn my mask
for so long now
I cannot take it off
I've worn my mask
for so long now
it's fused to my face
and time's painful stitches
make sure
it stays in place
I've worn my mask
for so long now
the scars are barely there
I do not tell them it's a mask
for no one really cares
I've worn my mask
for so long now
I am the mask I wear
To remove it
is impossible
for beneath it
I'm not there

Mark Bird

Fear

I am afraid, oh I am so afraid!
The cold black fear is clutching me to-night
As long ago when they would take the light
And leave the little child who would have prayed,
Frozen and sleepless at the thought of death.
My heart that beats too fast will rest too soon;
I shall not know if it be night or noon,
Yet shall I struggle in the dark for breath?
Will no one fight the Terror for my sake,
The heavy darkness that no dawn will break?
How can they leave me in that dark alone,
Who loved the joy of light and warmth so much,
And thrilled so with the sense of sound and touch,
How can they shut me underneath a stone?

Sara Teasdale

An Octopus Dwells Inside My Head

An octopus dwells inside my head,
And reaches for all the things I dread.
If I forget what's frightening me,
Its tentacles grasp more fears to see.

'Ignore the octopus in your head!'
At least that's what my therapist said.
But octopuses are wise, you see,
So perhaps it's watching out for me.

I tell myself this arrangement's fine,
I *need* this octopus in my mind.
Yet when it curls up and leaves me be,
I admit I'm freer to be me.

If you've an octopus in your head,
Whose suckers seek all the things you dread,
I understand and believe you're brave;
I hope in time it learns to behave.

As for this cephalopod of mine,
I think a compromise would be fine.
I'll let it wake up when danger's near –
Otherwise sleep, my octopus dear.

Cat Winters

Post

All I'm asking for
is a tolerable amount
of misery.

And maybe someone to love
as I continue to witness
the slow but gradual
dismantling
of everything I thought
I believed.

Matthew Freeman

What I Heard Her Say

with thanks to Kayleen

It is true, you are too much for some—
especially those who have not yet learned
they carry the sea inside them. Especially
those who still want to fit their lives
into small, dry boxes with tight-fitting tops.
But there will be some who desperately need you
to show up every bit as immense as you are,
not one drop smaller, need you to be unashamedly
vast and deep and full of strange things
neither you nor they can understand.
Maybe it's just one person who needs you
to be that big. Maybe that person is you.

Rosemerry Wahtola Trommer

if nothing else

perhaps you're right: the world is terrible
at best, irredeemable on all but the most sun-kissed of days,

but if nothing else, you are here.
if nothing else, that matters.

despite everything that has come before, and
everything yet to come – and it will come, it always does.

and perhaps you're right: we're all brittle things, really
built from afterimages and impressions:

wool snagging on barbed wire;
stones collecting in the bend of a river;
the glow of a camera flash after the light is
gone

and perhaps you're right: life is loss and the spaces between loss
and little else.

but if nothing else, there are spaces between.
and if nothing else, we are anything but brittle:

how could we be, when every wild joy and unutterable trauma
is knotted so inextricably into our skin?

presence as a product of absence.
absence as proof of presence.

nothing so brittle is a monument
to everything you have been before, and everything you are yet to
be

and the world is only ever irredeemable if you are.

Harry Woodgate

Here's what I'm afraid of

Doing the wrong thing,
Saying the wrong thing,
Not living life to its fullest potential,
Not having any potential,
Being too masculine,
Being too feminine,
Cutting my hair,
The greying of my hair,
And what it means, to grey,
Split ends (less a fear, and a minor inconvenience)
Stress levels / Cortisol
Having wasted my teens
Being in my twenties,
The thought of being in my forties,
fifties,
sixties
(and thirties)
Everything on TikTok
X
And Insta Reels
Because I just can't keep up . . .
My anxiety,
And the need to be perfect –
always
all the time

Everyone around hating me,
Being left out
Eating too much,
Eating too little,
My body,
How weak it is,
My muscle mass,
Taking things too far,
Not taking things far enough,
Loving too much,
Falling too quickly,
Loving too many,
Not loving anyone enough.
Not being loved enough.
Not being loved.
The world and how it's burning
The world and how it takes and takes and takes
The world and all that's in it
The world
The world
The world

Charlie Castelletti

The Ones Who Doubt You and The Ones Who Don't

Those who doubt you,
do not know you well enough to understand
how much you have been through,
they have not seen your scars.

Those who believe in you,
are the ones who know
how much you have had to endure
and how truly fearless you are.

Nikita Gill

I'M FEELING . . .
BLUE

Today Will Be Mostly Blue

not the cyan of summer
or sapphire crystals of snow
not the cornflower canvas
where spring embroiders swallows
or the bluebell footprints
of waking woods – no

not distant haze of mountain
or berry scent of gorse
not the shimmer of a raven
or the gleam of seal's wet coat
no more the ache of frozen fingers
or ghosts of drifting boats

not a bruised eye or winter
though that is something close
not the taste or the shape of it
not the shade of it or lack
no not really a colour
just this feeling I have

Sue Hardy-Dawson

Dissociation Is a Mental Process of Disconnecting from One's Thoughts, Feelings, Memories or Surroundings

The first time I saw sadness was from the air.

     I haven't been myself for a long time.

Feeling detached from my body in the space of an evening

     I display no emotion, opinion or reaction

it feels as though it never happened

     holding a conversation

has caused whole chunks of my life to disappear.

I know I went to high school

     as if I was seeing the world in a dream.

I'm a person trying my best to play 'me'

     when I'm uncertain if my arms are mine.

If my body is present, people tend to expect

     the rest of me to be too.

Is anyone ever completely in the room?

     We all end up in places and

don't know how we got there.

Shauna Darling Robertson

The Blues

When the shoe strings break
On both your shoes
And you're in a hurry –
That's the blues.

When you go to buy a candy bar
And you've lost the dime you had –
Slipped through a hole in your pocket somewhere –
That's the blues, too, and bad!

Langston Hughes

The Depression Trail

Take a left at the last road sign
and walk into the lush wood.

Follow the trail called Depression.
Your shadow touches the shade

of these knotted, unbending trees
and your borrowed compass wobbles

then doesn't stop spinning. No signal
out here. Your watch has packed in.

The car park map didn't mention this route
didn't give an estimated completion time.

Welly weather. Rain coming in sideways
hailstones scratching your new glasses.

Keep moving. Trudge through muck.
Mind ditches, branches in the ground.

There's life on this poxy path. Look.
Black Ladybirds on every tree trunk.

Some people think this trail isn't real.
Tell that to my soaked-through Doc Martens

Tell that to the caked-in mud in my soles
the worm I accidentally stepped on, you think.

Notice the painted signpost telling you
A river with a mouthful name is up ahead.

Before you go on, spot the brushwork
mould resistant, unsmudged, cursive.

I bet you think the water's polluted.
Think again. It's clear as the school bell.

By the bank, your childhood bed,
the stickers from cereal boxes still

on the red frame. Lay down. Stretch.
The sky will be empty some days.

Stare long enough and you'll see
the constant drift of shapeless clouds

saying soon, soon you'll reach a clearing
follow a desire line out of here

make a new untrodden trail.
You're no fool. You know full well

when you leave, your feet will remember
the trail that no sat-nav can find.

Maybe you'll find yourself back here
by chance, mistake or fate, depending

on who you ask. You'll be older
than you ever thought possible.

The wilting leaves will go on telling
their hushed tales, this early dark

will carry on searching for your footprints
and try to get at the holes in your boots.

The rows of dead men's fingers will keep
reaching up for the birdhouses you built.

Someone will trace your steps.
But all that can wait for now.

Stay a while. Watch the stream.
Sit. Feel what you need to feel.

Karl Knights

Internet Friendship

You still appear in my Friends list,
as if the Internet does not know
that you're dead.

Although your status has been stuck
on 'grey', and now it no longer
bothers to record how many hours ago

you were last active. Somebody
has changed your name to
'In Memory Of', so all your photos

of Disneyland and pumpkin patches
aren't deleted. I don't know about
anyone else, but some nights

I delve back through DMs
that now gather dust, to listen again
to your voice notes. The time difference

never daunted you – you'd take
an unauthorized break mid-shift
to perch on a shut toilet lid

and whisper 'Happy New Year'
to me across whole oceans.
When I get a new phone, I still add

your numbers to my contacts,
its glamorous and alien dialling code,
the '001626' preening its odd beauty

between the doctors, the landlord,
the local taxi. One day, maybe,
it will appear on my screen,

some call from beyond to say
it was a joke that got
out of hand, and did you miss me?

Maybe not. I keep you
on my Close Friends list,
just in case,

although there's nothing
I can do for your Sims.
They must circle forever

in the black-box server, masterless
and probably bored, but safe there,
snug in pixels beyond

any meteors or deleted pool ladders
that would summon
a tiny animated Grim Reaper,

nudged into service
by a click of your keys,
uncontrolled by a now-absent God.

Betty Doyle

Breaking Down the Blues

Sometimes when I'm feeling blue
I try to figure out the hue
like it's a painter's palette I can feel:
a funk that at first glance I think'll
be a shade of periwinkle
actually turns out to be a teal.

Babies get the baby blues, and Kaiser Bill got Prussian blues,
but when you look straight at them they're less likely to be crushing
    blues.

I could try and tell for hours if I'm *powder* blue or *sky* blue,
And *your* blue is never, ever quite the same as *my* blue –

The next time that you've got the blues, why don't you try the same
and see if you can narrow down your feeling to a name:

Are you feeling sort of Robin's-Egg-ly? Or maybe bright Sapphire-ly?
Aquamarine or Ultramarine or some other Marine entirely?
If your mind is in Electric Blue, you might just get a shock,
like when I find I'm feeling Midnight Blue but it's only five o'clock.

Are you Navy Blue or Royal Blue, Cerulean or Cyan?
Moroccan Blue, Egyptian Blue, or Bristol Blue, or Mayan?

Blue like the sky,
blue like an eye,
blue like the inside of blueberry pie?
Blue like the buzz of a bluebottle fly?
Blue like a pair of blue suede shoes that have just been newly
    shined?

Oh, you're feeling *green*?
Then never mind.

Daniel Galef

I felt a Funeral, in my Brain

I felt a Funeral, in my Brain,
And Mourners to and fro
Kept treading – treading – till it seemed
That Sense was breaking through –

And when they all were seated,
A Service, like a Drum –
Kept beating – beating – till I thought
My Mind was going numb –

And then I heard them lift a Box
And creak across my Soul
With those same Boots of Lead, again,
Then Space – began to toll,

As all the Heavens were a Bell,
And Being, but an Ear,
And I, and Silence, some strange Race,
Wrecked, solitary, here –

And then a Plank in Reason, broke,
And I dropped down, and down –
And hit a World, at every plunge,
And Finished knowing – then –

Emily Dickinson

Away Message

I would like to tell you where I've been.

I would like to tell you I've been fighting ninjas over San Francisco. Dangerous ones with blades and expert marksmanship and I've been in mortal danger.

I would like to tell you I've been holed up in hiding because I've learned terrible secrets of the universe, whispered to me by a mystical beast in a dark cave late at night.

I would like to tell you I've been swimming with the mermaids off the icy coasts of Greenland and my fingers have been too numbed by their scaly fins and seaweed hair to type.

I would like to tell you these interesting things.

They are not true.

I am sad.

Times are hard.

Imagination is fickle.

We are taught to say "thank you for your patience" when we want to say "I'm sorry" because we're learning, as a generation, to forgive ourselves.

Thank you for your patience.

MJ Huntsgood

Poem for a Pebble

I found you on a sad day.

You lay on the pavement's edge
as if someone had kicked you aside,

small, grey and imperfectly round.
Eyes to the ground, I crept past,

then a flicker of su', and you winked
an' I *knew* that wink was for me.

You were a perfect fit for my palm
and, close up, so much more

than just grey, with starry sprinkles
of pink and cream,

shiny and pitted, smooth and rough
all at the same time.

You made me think
about the zillions of years

it took to make you this way –
still inside you, the spit of volcanos

the cold toes of glaciers,
the wild-beating heart of the sea.

You are the secret 'I hol'
in the snug darkness of pockets.

How warm you grow
as you take my sadness away.

Victoria Gatehouse

Sad

I've done sad.
I've mastered it.

Explored each crevice and scoured
each record in its tear-soaked library.
Named it: desolation, woe, pity, despair,
called out each one to judge and jury –
made sure each offence was known –
swallowed tinctures and sought counsel,
wrung my hands at the Tragedy of Life,
put my picture next to maudlin in the dictionary,
and now . . .

I'm bored.

So whilst I'm able to
(and whilst it's true)
I'd like to try

Something new.

Annabelle Sami

That Time of the Month Again

My downwards spiral could be predicted from a long ways off
if I cared to count that far into the future.
I don't want to number my days when they're already numbered,
so I let the dark torpor and general bad-temperedness,
the collapse into tears and lonely self-pitying moments,
take me unexpected yet another time.
How suddenly it all dragged me down,
as I lay on my stomach with a pillow under my abdomen
thinking of all the things that make me despicable.
It does no good to tell myself I should be happy
when my own sly blood is telling me to cry.

M. Stevenson

I'M FEELING . . .
GRIEF

I measure every Grief I meet

I measure every Grief I meet
With narrow, probing, Eyes –
I wonder if It weighs like Mine –
Or has an Easier size.

I wonder if They bore it long –
Or did it just begin –
I could not tell the Date of Mine –
It feels so old a pain –

I wonder if it hurts to live –
And if They have to try –
And whether – could They choose between –
It would not be – to die –

I note that Some – gone patient long –
At length, renew their smile –
An imitation of a Light
That has so little Oil –

I wonder if when Years have piled –
Some Thousands – on the Harm –
That hurt them early – such a lapse
Could give them any Balm –

Or would they go on aching still
Through Centuries of Nerve –
Enlightened to a larger Pain –
In Contrast with the Love –

The Grieved – are many – I am told –
There is the various Cause –
Death – is but one – and comes but once –
And only nails the eyes –

There's Grief of Want – and Grief of Cold –
A sort they call 'Despair' –
There's Banishment from native Eyes –
In sight of Native Air –

And though I may not guess the kind –
Correctly – yet to me
A piercing Comfort it affords
In passing Calvary –

To note the fashions – of the Cross –
And how they're mostly worn –
Still fascinated to presume
That Some – are like My Own –

Emily Dickinson

Love/Loss

Scientists have recently proven what poets have always known:
Love and heartbreak both write themselves on your body.
Your cells, your brain, they change when you love someone.
When you lose them, they shift even more.
Heartache is an earthquake,
a shaking of your very self,
until so much that seemed steady is broken.
In the rubble of your love,
In the desolation of your grief,
Perhaps you can find something to hold on to.
A piece of who you've lost—
Best friend, first love, family, or even a piece of who you once were—
And from that small piece you can build something new.
Something more beautiful than you ever imagined.
Though it will still hurt of course.
Grief doesn't go away because we ask it to.
Things end. People leave. It's terrible and true, but it's also
     something we share.
Perhaps in sharing that loss, we can heal from it.
Perhaps we can make peace with our changed cells, our broken
     hearts, our toppled futures.
I hope so, at least.

Jamie Pacton

~ on grief ~

sometimes it will feel
like time has stopped
for no one else but
you
like you are being
pulled
apart
by
forces
beyond your control.

let it.

sometimes it will feel
like being crushed
under an infinite weight
trying to escape
the ravenous dark
that's dragging you in
while everyone else
is safe behind
the point of
no return.

don't be afraid.

of going through
the black hole
while cradled by stars
and trust that
it will lead you
to the light waiting
for you
on the other side

Cora Dessalines

Echo

Come to me in the silence of the night;
　　Come in the speaking silence of a dream;
Come with soft rounded cheeks and eyes as bright
　　As sunlight on a stream;
　　　Come back in tears,
O memory, hope, love of finished years.

O dream how sweet, too sweet, too bitter sweet,
　　Whose wakening should have been in Paradise,
Where souls brimfull of love abide and meet;
　　Where thirsting longing eyes
　　　Watch the slow door
That opening, letting in, lets out no more.

Yet come to me in dreams, that I may live
　　My very life again though cold in death:
Come back to me in dreams, that I may give
　　Pulse for pulse, breath for breath:
　　　Speak low, lean low
As long ago, my love, how long ago.

Christina Rossetti

Grief
Moves in and rearranges the furniture
Takes control of the remote
holding your hand all the while

Even on the sunniest of days
Breaking the most gentle of your favorite china

It holds on to your ability to spread
Your wings, clinging to your Psyche

No poem suffices
No/ space in between the cracks
It climbs on your back
Dragging you/knuckles to ground

Isn't it a strange rainbow
The dark delineated designs in a kaleidoscope/ where
    the deepest love/
is now
fractured/hollowed out/ & distorted

I look at the sky in those confines,

Seeing colors and reliving shapes
    grateful
For the grief I carry

There was love
to be mourned here
Joy to be had
Depression to Overcome
A hero's tale to be told

To see that I have sunsets
With my name engraved in them
I find gratitude
in the intricacies of this weighted grief
mourning so many
versions and visions of me, us, we's and you's

Lysz Flo

The Night Where You No Longer Live

Was it like lifting a veil
And was the grass treacherous, the green grass

Did you think of your own mother

Was it like a virus
Did the software flicker

And was this the beginning
Was it like that

Was there gas station food

       and was it a long trip

And is there sun there
or drones
or punishment
or growth

Was it a blackout

And did you still create me
And what was I like on the first day of my life

Were we two from the start
And was our time an entrance
   or an ending

Did we stand in the heated room
Did we look at the painting

Did the snow appear cold
Were our feet red with it, with the wet snow

And then what were our names
Did you love me or did I misunderstand

     Is it terrible

Do you intend to come back

Do you hear the world's keening

Will you stay the night

Meghan O'Rourke

The Three Deaths
For Pop

Have you ever heard the theory of the three deaths?
The first is when the body dies
Which is sad
That is when we lose you
But there is comfort there too
No more fear
No more pain
No more loneliness
Just peace
Just comfort
Surrounded by those you had loved and lost
Say hello from us

The second visual, when we say goodbye
Which is hard
This is when we see your shell one last time
But we get to celebrate you
We tell stories
We see old photos
Photos we'd forgotten or never seen before
You're not in the casket, but you're here
We'll close the lid
We'll throw the dirt
See you no more
But your hand is on our shoulders

Third . . . the third I'll never see
I'll never have to mourn a third
The third, you see, is not until you are forgotten
And I will never forget you
We did not lose you at the first death
We will still be with you after the second
And you will live every time I open up my sunroof
You breathe every time I pick up a wooden toy
Your heart beats every time mine beats

You live through me
In me
With me
Until I join you.
Now, I know you don't want that too soon
Neither do I
I have places to take your memory . . .
But when the day comes
I take comfort knowing you're saving me a seat.

I love you.
See you then.

C. T. Wood

The Debt

This is the debt I pay
Just for one riotous day,
Years of regret and grief,
Sorrow without relief.

Pay it I will to the end –
Until the grave, my friend,
Gives me a true release –
Gives me the clasp of peace.

Slight was the thing I bought,
Small was the debt I thought,
Poor was the loan at best —
God! but the interest!

Paul Laurence Dunbar

On Landing and Leaving Home

It's like –
that space between the car door and pavement.
Like expecting another step when there isn't one.
Or missing a step entirely. Like
the sound of keys turning in the lock but it's only
next-door, filling elsewhere with life
and that particular smell of skin in summer.

Coming back from your favourite pub smelling sweetly of fried
    food and beer.
Dancing sweaty in a London bar hours after leaving Albania.
Sleeping on your sister's divan alongside your wife and her
    scattered heart.
Calling home from a London payphone: red dilapidated matchbox.
Sneaking into Electric Cinema for your favourite film,
    misunderstanding.
Walking along Portobello Road smelling pancakes, two perfect ice
    cream scoops.
A warm waffle.
Watching steam morph into cigarette smoke in stiff air, daydreaming.

It's snowing back home, knee-high white, says your mother,
sad through the static phone line after your wife tells you she's
    pregnant,
heart breaking in the borrowed red skirt-suit, her sister's.

Like that gulf over the kitchen counter
between the two of you once the last bag is unpacked and this is home.

But you were expecting another step. The click of the car door as it
unlocks. The jolt of the plane landing. A carriage in December.

Dredhëza Maloku

Remember

Remember me when I am gone away,
　　· Gone far away into the silent land;
　　When you can no more hold me by the hand,
Nor I half turn to go yet turning stay.
Remember me when no more day by day
　　You tell me of our future that you plann'd:
　　Only remember me; you understand
It will be late to counsel then or pray.
Yet if you should forget me for a while
　　And afterwards remember, do not grieve:
　　For if the darkness and corruption leave
　　A vestige of the thoughts that once I had,
Better by far you should forget and smile
　　Than that you should remember and be sad.

Christina Rossetti

I'M FEELING . . .

LOST OR CONFUSED, OR LIKE I NEED HELP

An Ordinary Day

I took my mind a walk
or my mind took me a walk –
whichever was the truth of it.

The light glittered on the water
or the water glittered in the light.
Cormorants stood on a tidal rock

with their wings spread out,
stopping no traffic. Various ducks
shilly-shallied here and there

on the shilly-shallying water.
An occasional gull yelped. Small flowers
were doing their level best

to bring to their kerb bees like
aerial charabancs. Long weeds in the clear
water did Eastern dances, unregarded

by shoals of darning needles. A cow
started a moo but thought
better of it . . . And my feet took me home

and my mind observed to me,
or I to it, how ordinary
extraordinary things are or

how extraordinary ordinary
things are, like the nature of the mind
and the process of observing.

Norman MacCaig

There's No One Else Like Me

There's no one else like me.
There's no one else who's
sad like me
embarrassed like me
lonely like me
ashamed like me
anxious like me
clumsy like me
stupid like me
confused like me
angry like me.

Except

my mum when she was my age
my dad when he was my age
my gran when she was my age
my teacher, who tells us stories
about when she was a goth
and most of my friends.

There's no one else like me.
There's no one else who really
understands people who are

sad
embarrassed
lonely
ashamed
anxious
clumsy
stupid
confused
angry.

Except

my mum (sometimes)
my dad (sometimes)
my gran (always)
my teacher (when the class behaves)
and, of course,

most of my friends.

Barbara Bleiman

Elemental

Somewhere in
the house a
pipe drips –
shards
of metal
exposed
to air

It reminds me
that even
steel gives
way over
time

Worn down
by the
relentless
pressure
of water

Give yourself
grace

Clara Elena García

Loss and Gain

When I compare
What I have lost with what I have gained,
What I have missed with what attained,
   Little room do I find for pride.

I am aware
How many days have been idly spent;
How like an arrow the good intent
   Has fallen short or been turned aside.

But who shall dare
To measure loss and gain in this wise?
Defeat may be victory in disguise;
   The lowest ebb is the turn of the tide.

Henry Wadsworth Longfellow

Not So Dear Diary

Monday: anxious

Tuesday: bad

Wednesday: grumpy

Thursday: sad

Friday: euphoric – don't know why. I can do anything! Watch me fly!

Weekend: cringe at Friday's clowning – urgh! Wish I could die!

Kate Williams

Age Fourteen, Online Quiz

do you feel confused about your sexual orientation?

to say *yes* seems too simple   what i am
is foreign   to my own feelings
& indecisive   & gorged with want
begging   for a trap door
to yank me   into another dimension

if a girl flirted with you, what would your reaction be?

                because i'm a ~~growl~~ girl   & shy   & awkward
                        my face would turn stovetop   my hands
                                vibrating   by my sides   an urge
                        to reach out   & pinch my arm   to see
                                                if i was dreaming

do you feel sexually attracted to girls?

how to define *sexual attraction*
but as pulsing nerves   chest
sensation sharp   as a whiff of jasmine
a perfume   my favorite scent

do you have any fantasies or dreams of having
sexual relations with a girl?

but will it sound gay   to answer *often*
so much harder to   control
unconscious thoughts
last night i dreamed   a manicured hand
made its way   up my skirt
it was so warm   & so soft

have you touched yourself imagining it was a girl?

in a word   *yes*   i shut my eyes
breathe heavy   picture that hand
another pulsing body beneath me
skin soft as a peach   & as ripe

have you had sexual relations with a girl?

think back to the night   in the bathroom
~~a girl & a growl~~ two girls   long after sundown
her hand   on my thigh
my fingers threading   through her hair
gusts of wind   no   breath

do you feel sexually aroused when being touched by a girl?

pulsing nerves   chest
sharp   as a whiff of jasmine
a familiar scent   & sensation
like the creek   running
through the forest   i can almost reach out

                              & touch

                         Despy Boutris

A learned man came to me once

A learned man came to me once.
He said: 'I know the way, — come.'
And I was overjoyed at this.
Together we hastened.
Soon, too soon, were we
Where my eyes were useless,
And I knew not the ways of my feet.
I clung to the hand of my friend;
But at last he cried, 'I am lost.'

Stephen Crane

The Bully

Are you ready to hear about a break-up story,
exposing a bully in all his glory?
See there was this guy that I used to know,
he wasn't exactly my Romeo,
I wasn't his Juliet and he wasn't my friend
though we nearly came to a similar end . . .

I meet him when I'm just a little girl,
feeling a bit different from the others and also way too short for
    this world –
Don't worry, I grew – though barely past five foot two,
sorry I digress, I do that sometimes
find it hard to control the thoughts in my mind . . .

So I'm a young girl and I meet this lad,
the thing is at the start he wasn't that bad,
the thing is there's a part of me that was glad
that he stood by me, helped protect what I had.

I'd get mad yeah
When I was a teen.
I'd get scared by the way that the world seemed to be.
But what now is controlling, back then was barely there
just the occasional behavior that would make me less scared.
He'd tell me what to do, tell me how to survive.

But pretty soon if I didn't obey he would eat me alive.

What if this? What if that?
What happens then?
I'll make sure nothing bad if you just count to ten.
Do it again and then do it again,
avoid this, just touch that, fingers crossed and amen.
But the more I listened the more bad thoughts would stem and
    condemn me
all his commands disguised as helping.

I grow older and he grows louder,
I try to be bold but he's shouting me down.
Negating, degrading me,
suffocating my brain and he
rarely shuts up and it's irritating and paining me.
A cycle of fear then instruction and fear then instruction,
makes me see harmless things with a view of repulsion.
And not much can be done when his voice gets this strong,
and my thoughts are obsessing over obsessive compulsions.
And it's no fun, man,
I'm done, man,
I want to break up.
But when I'm scared he comes back, knows just what's up.

But after a while I hear that this thing has a name,
that I'm not the only one with a bully in my brain.

That it's common –
Well like one in a hundred –
that there are ways to beat him and those ways are abundant.
This repugnant, fun-sucking creature that's mugging me
of all of my logic, he doesn't have to be permanent.
Knowledge is power is the fact of the hour,
And guess what? I like reading
about ways to defeat him.

Understanding diagnosis is the first step to recovery,
making the choice that I won't let him smother me.
The decision to fight is the first step to victory,
knowing recovery's coming I'm unlocking the mystery.
He's history I don't need him
to be complete.
I learn how to stand on my own two feet.
And sometimes I might wobble if I think about before-me,
But I'm safe in the knowledge that I won't let him floor me
anymore now. I've learned to be strong though he told me I
    couldn't
and I'll keep moving forward because I'm pretty damn stubborn.
Sometimes he might pipe up, try to make me forget,
how badly he treated me
but I know now I deserve better.

Lucy Burke

At Low Tide

I go to the sea.

      Tell me what you know, I whisper to waves who have no
time to stop and talk.

They never do.
I think that's why I go there with all my questions.

None of us want the answers,
do we?

      We just want to go on,
despite it all.

We want to carry what we can and leave the rest
like the tides.

Christina Gessler

Good Listener

everyone keeps asking how I am
but what can I say?

If I say I'm sad, they say
I should be thankful I'm still here.

If I say I'm doing OK, they say
that's surprising after what I've been through.

If I say I'm angry, they say
I should've been more careful.

If I say I don't know how I am, they say
I should talk more.

But no one wants to listen.
Apart from you.

You're the only one I can talk to.
You're a good listener for a tree.

Stephen Lightbown

Crew

Are you feeling lonely?
That's OK, me too.

Are you shimmering on the shoreline
A single SOS
Waiting for the world to come back home?
Or do you think you were left
With supplies, a threadbare blanket
At someone's behest?
And the world, the world, just *left*
And moved on without you?
That's OK. Me too.

Do you think about the clouds like ships
Like the hands and white boxes
On street-corners? Shared secrets,
Shared chips. That's OK. I get it.
Fingertips and ketchup packets
Handed out with zero care
As easily as texts and someone's hair
Turned into a moving image
For someone, somewhere
To laugh over. Not you.
You're *never* there.

Are you ever nervous? Stammering
On the inside, over the sound
Of your own laughter, jack-hammering
Like a newborn colt? The pound
Your feet make, over grass
Before they said *You walk too fast.*
It's not your fault.
It's not your fault.

Are you feeling stupid?
That's OK, me too.

Have you watched them come,
Then go? That's OK.
Me too.

Have you planned the pirate ship
That your brother built with you?
Sailed the seas, hands empty
And heart-head split in two?
Had flags unwound and lowered
By a solo drink or two? Have you sat
And sung (*spoken*) to this
Empty room?
Me too.
Have you sailed toward survival?
That's OK. Me too!

Have you found yourself, unseeing
And found new worlds? Me too!
Have you loved yourself, in sunlight?
In sand, shade? (Tell me to.)
Have you found yourself surviving?

. . . That's OK. Me too.

Eleanor Powell

Take Care

Take care of the flowers.
Although you can't see their colours right now,
they'll be waiting for you
when you return.

And mend the roof.
Right now you're drenched
from lashings of rain,
but the time will soon come

when you finally step
into the warmth.
A shelter will be waiting for you,
and the beautiful colours outside.

Take care now, even though
it all feels empty, hopeless.
Good things await you,
and you will see that life is good.

Joshua Seigal

Subtext

When are you back?

How are you getting home?

Have you eaten?

Who's going?

And where?

I saw it as nagging,
but now know she meant;

Life's fragile.

You're precious.

I care.

Sarah Ziman

I'M FEELING . . .

IN NEED OF YOUR WISDOM

felt

jeez o.
language.
what's it like.
on and on.
blahdyblah.
i don't know.
feelings but.
feelings eh
just leave them be
just . . .

. . .

hold your tongue
just

. . .

let them be felt

Stewart Ennis

Message to the 14-Year-Old Me

Believe in yourself.
You can do anything you set your heart on –
except A level physics, perhaps.
Well, all the sciences really.

DIY is a bit of a no-no, too.
See also: driving; skiing, map-reading;
cooking pasta in the right quantities;
relationships; origami.

Don't even think about running
your own business. Or singing in tune.
Best to steer clear of all activities which require
good hand-eye coordination.

Forget ice-skating, tending house plants,
dealing with spiders, the correct spelling of the word
'enjambement'. I could go on.
But do not despair – for given time

and with a little luck on your side –
you can achieve a basic level of competence
in a limited number of simple, unremarkable things,
you just need to believe in yourself

Brian Bilston

Sensitive

S-E-N-S-I-T-I-V-E
they use this word like a terrible, horrible curse. like it's so bad
to feel deeply until there's nothing left to be felt. i should hold
my head high, stop letting words crush my core, shut my feelings
off until i run dry, leaving an empty hole in my heart where water
once lied. i don't think they understand feeling nothing at all is
worse than feeling everything. because it's these unexplainable,
unnameable feelings that pulse in my chest that remind me every
day that i'm breathing, that i'm living, that i'm someone in the
world who exists outside of myself.

Raye Halabuza

Love and Friendship

Love is like the wild rose-brier;
　　Friendship like the holly-tree.
The holly is dark when the rose-brier blooms,
　　But which will bloom most constantly?

The wild rose-brier is sweet in spring,
　　Its summer blossoms scent the air;
Yet wait till winter comes again,
　　And who will call the wild-brier fair!

Then, scorn the silly rose-wreath now,
　　And deck thee with the holly's sheen,
That, when December blights thy brow,
　　He still may leave thy garland green.

Emily Brontë

A Love Letter

Dear Tortured Soul,

I'm here to tell you that you are worthy.

You are beautiful beyond measure.

You are one of a kind.

It's true . . . the world will try to break you down, tearing you apart piece by piece until all that's left is your raw essence – the bones of who you truly are.

How do I know? *I've been there*. I've been through the gamut of emotion, the trial by fire that is teenage life. And I'm here to say it gets better. I promise.

I remember being tempted by the endless dark, by the sharp kiss of possibility . . . but I implore you! Push those thoughts down. Stomp on them. Beat them with your fists. Scream. *Rebel!*

Because there is beauty in the breakdown.

Hardship grows character and sooner than you can imagine you'll burst through the darkness of your despair and the sunlight will shine down on you. For though the world is cruel, it's beautiful in the truest sense and so much more awaits you!

Your heart will know love, empathy, and compassion. You'll be understanding; a champion of those who are hurting – because *you* have been there.

And yes, as someone who's lived on the fringes, never a part of the crowd, but something other . . . you might be jaded, *but embrace it*. Embrace the pain, the joy, the good, and the bad. Your experiences create you like a potter molds their clay.

And you are still being molded. You'll never stop.

But one day, years from now, you're going to look back at your life and you're going to be proud of who you are. Your journey might've been a difficult one, but nothing worthwhile in life comes easy.

Fight to be you.

Fight to be here.

You are incredible and your story is only just beginning.

With love,
The Future.

Raven Wildwood

A Golden Shovel At Heartbreak Hotel

Nothing is ever as hopeless as it seems. Look,

down here, where the crocuses are rioting around

the broken glass, gold as yolks in cracked earth. And there, at

the splintered eye socket that used to be our window, see how

the magpies are nesting, hoarding photographs and mattress

    springs, lucky

and loud mouthed as pirate kings. Here's the thing, we

owe it to ourselves not to let winter win this war. There are

so many things worth rebuilding for, only to

fall hand in hand all over again – this most exquisite cycle. To be

here, now, in this rubble-strewn skin, with every nerve-ending alive

to the future and its beckoning thresholds. That's something, right?

It starts with laying a single stone. It starts now.

The end word of each line are lyrics from 'That Would Be Enough'
from Hamilton by Lin-Manuel Miranda

Jen Feroze

Leaving the Tate

Coming out with your clutch of postcards
in a Tate Gallery bag and another clutch
of images packed into your head you pause
on the steps to look across the river

and there's a new one: light bright buildings,
a streak of brown water, and such a sky
you wonder who painted it – Constable? No:
too brilliant. Crome? No: too ecstatic –

a madly pure Pre-Raphaelite sky,
perhaps, sheer blue apart from the white plumes
rushing up it (today, that is,
April. Another day would be different

but it wouldn't matter. All skies work.)
Cut to the lower right for a detail:
seagulls pecking on mud, below
two office blocks and a Georgian terrace.

Now swing to the left, and take in plane trees
bobbled with seeds, and that brick building,
and a red bus . . . Cut it off just there,
by the lamp-post. Leave the scaffolding in.

That's your next one. Curious how
these outdoor pictures didn't exist
before you'd looked at the indoor pictures,
the ones on the walls. But here they are now,

marching out of their panorama
and queuing up for the viewfinder
your eye's become. You can isolate them
by holding your optic muscles still.

You can zoom in on figure studies
(that boy with the rucksack), or still lives,
abstracts, townscapes. No one made them.
The light painted them. You're in charge

of the hanging committee. Put what space
you like around the ones you fix on,
and gloat. Art multiplies itself.
Art's whatever you choose to frame.

Fleur Adcock

Lemons

When life gives you lemons
make lemonade
or just feel a bit sour for a while.

When life gives you lemons
make a lemon drizzle cake
or have a cry.

When life gives you lemons
invite your friends round
to make lemon meringue pie
or go to bed with your phone.

When life gives you lemons
think about lemons and life.

If you want to.

Rob Walton

The Whole Oak

The whole oak
is too much
for the acorn to contain –

the sea's sound-surge
too huge
for the shell's chamber.

The rainbow
is too bright to spring
from sunlight and clear glass

and yet
   the truth remains

the self contains

too much, and
just enough.

   Imogen Russell Williams

This Is a Shout Out

to the silent –
who, when asked if they would rather
ham or cheese, rain or shine, win or lose,
could manage only
don't mind
or *you choose* –
who sat and sipped a half of mild
for everyone else's pint of bitter
and who bit down,
buttoned in,
battened down,
bottled up,
stood only on ceremony
and never once stepped on toes –
who, early on, perfected the process
of folding themselves into neat little pieces
and learned how to leave a room empty
by entering it –
who repackaged themselves so tightly
they would never again come apart
and who still
take the librarian's *hush*
to heart.

Shauna Darling Robertson

On Her Fifteenth Birthday, I Tell My Sister Why a Woman is Like a Bouquet of Flowers

I want to give you something
you will not need pockets to carry.
At your age, I held two languages
in my mouth and swallowed one by accident,
a tooth lost in the night.
What will you end up regretting?
Already, you confide a dissatisfaction
with the body that moves you through this world.
I want you to know, there are reasons
for me to worry about you.
Consider this: we cut flowers
because we think they're beautiful,
their petals so soft,
and easily bruised.

Megan J. Arlett

Show Them

Show them what it means to be astounding
Show them magic made real
They didn't know who you were
So show them.

Show them you can blow hurricanes with a breath
And carve canyons with a heel.
They didn't know you're mighty
So show them.

Show them strength in tenderness
Show them how to feel
Tidal tears and tempests heal
So show them.

Show your heart as you look in the mirror
That though ache is all it knows
The times you've felt the sharpest pain
Is when you needed most to grow.

Show the one who left you behind
(Or who, behind, you left)
You were forged to survive
There's gold inside your chest.

No matter what the crowds decide
No matter how stacked the odds

They don't know who you are
So show them.

Annabelle Sami

Bring a Coat

When no one talks to you, read your book. And, when they do, put the book down and talk to them. Don't get coloured bands in braces. Dye your hair red, pink and purple. Just not at the same time. Don't laugh at things you don't find funny, especially from boys you don't find funny. If you're known as the mad girl, lean into it. When they ask you about it – wanting every gory detail – tell them to fuck off. You don't owe everyone the truth or your truth. Pack. If he tells you you looked better blonde, remember you looked better single. Kiss her. Patience is overrated. Move to London. Say yes. When they don't promote you, ask why. When they promote you, ask for more money. Pack. Don't date Tories. Make a scene. Wee after sex. Kiss him. Pack. Wear lipstick, lots of it. If you don't want to be friends with her, don't be. Buy a nice coat, one that will last for a few years. Say no. Speak up. A job interview is the perfect time to take a feminist stance. If they don't talk to you, ask them what they're reading. Tell your cat you love him. Tell your mum you love her. Move again.

Unpack. Bring a coat.

Charlotte Moore

Life

A crust of bread and a corner to sleep in,
A minute to smile and an hour to weep in,
A pint of joy to a peck of trouble,
And never a laugh but the moans come double;
          And that is life!

A crust and a corner that love makes precious,
With a smile to warm and the tears to refresh us;
And joy seems sweeter when cares come after,
And a moan is the finest of foils for laughter;
          And that is life!

Paul Laurence Dunbar

Index of First Lines

"Hope" is the thing with feathers   84

A crust of bread and a corner to sleep in   237

A girl and her mother, holding hands   103

A learned man came to me once   207

A little Heartbreak, wan and sore   41

A thousand miles away a country burns   65

A voice bursts through, whispering for destruction   24

After your heart breaks   43

All I'm asking for   147

Am I too much?   xxi

An octopus dwells inside my head   146

Anxiety as a trans person feels heightened   63

Are you feeling lonely?   213

Are you ready to hear about a break-up story   208

At lunchtime I bought a huge orange   124

because the world didn't end when i came out as bisexual   85

Believe in yourself   222

Come to me in the silence of the night   182

Coming out with your clutch of postcards   228

Dear poetry editor   68

Dear Tortured Soul   225

do you feel confused about your sexual orientation?   204

Doing the wrong thing   151

Even tonight and I need to take a walk and clear   28

everyone keeps asking how I am   212

Finding entrances with friends   56

Finding exits in cramped rooms   54

Good news waits   81

Grief moves in and rearranges the furniture   183

Have you ever heard the theory of the three deaths?   187

He sees red everywhere   19

I am a gorilla   60

I am afraid, oh I am so afraid!   145

I am alone   94

I am happy   126

I am standing   142

I am the aftermath of the stars   11

I am too angry at the world   30

I am trying on happiness   128

i don't want to admit it   5

I drink green tea by my seedlings   37

I felt a Funeral, in my Brain   168

I found you on a sad day   170

I go to the sea   211

I love all shining things   125

I loved you first: but afterwards your love   12

I measure every Grief I meet   177

I read on the science of touch   9

I still call your mobile to hear your voice   114

I take the plunge   59

I tend the mobile now   15

I think I have to write this down	116
I thought of you and how you love this beauty	107
I took my mind a walk	197
I want ! to want ! to live !	58
I want to give you something	233
I was angry with my friend	27
I wish in the city of your heart	10
I would like to tell you where I've been	169
I'll have you smothered n covered n	3
I'm a hypocrite sometimes	64
I'm going to be a leaf today	77
I'm king and queen of this court	25
i'm scared of being nothing	139
I'm suddenly taken aback	104
I've been thinking about the way, when you walk	83
I've done sad	172
I've got a knot in my stomach	52
I've worn my mask	144
If I can stop one Heart from breaking	36
If I can't walk that fast	92
if stands for	71
If you suddenly and unexpectedly feel joy	134
In the gaps between	xix
It is true, you are too much for some	148
It's like	190
it's too late to remember what I came to Tesco for	115
jeez o	221

Later our salt and pepper cat   113

let it ache, let it hurt, let it sting   46

Let's be arsonists   29

Love is like the wild rose-brier   224

Marathons and races have pace-setters   90

Me: Gran, where did you first meet Grandpa?   101

Monday: anxious   203

My downwards spiral could be predicted from a long ways off 173

My imp comes with me everywhere I go   62

Not a red rose or a satin heart   13

not the cyan of summer   157

Nothing is ever as hopeless as it seems   227

O, were I loved as I desire to be!   4

Oh, I forgot to tell you!   78

Open up, you say   69

perhaps you're right: the world is terrible   149

Remember me when I am gone away   192

Rose, for the blooms that drew me in   20

Scientists have recently proven what poets have always known 179

S-E-N-S-I-T-I-V-E   223

she tells me her favourite flowers are sunflowers   99

She wore a new 'terra-cotta' dress   106

Show them what it means to be astounding   234

Something finally clicked over in my brain   82

sometimes it will feel   180

Sometimes when I stand   110

Sometimes when I'm feeling blue   166

Sometimes you are going to miss a person   40
Somewhere in the house   201
Square teeth gummed   22
Take a left at the last road sign   160
Take care of the flowers   216
Take my heart   35
That I matter   42
The first time I saw sadness was from the air   158
the future is a diffuse light   80
The ocean floor is where the darkest, coldest things go to   39
The summer Frank Ocean dropped Channel Orange   108
The whole oak   231
There is no word   51
There is, of course, that first momentous rip   45
There's no one else like me   199
They fuck you up, your mum and dad   21
This is a shout out to the silent   232
This is me, laughing   130
This is the debt I pay   189
This is what it looks like when   141
This, too, will pass   93
Those who doubt you   153
Today yes is made of lead   89
Travel through life   87
Was it like lifting a veil   185
we should have funerals for places   112
What a Joy It Is   132

When are you back?   217

When I compare   202

When life gives you lemons   230

When no one talks to you, read your book   236

When the shoe strings break   159

You are angry and anxious   26

You know, if you got to know me, I think you'd like me   140

You still appear in my Friends list   163

You're never too poor to give away kindness   73

You're telling me to smile   123

Your heart, a wild and untamed thing   7

Index of Poets and Translators

Adcock, Fleur	228
Ahmed, Munira Tabassum	80
Alejandra, Christina	xxi
Arlett, Megan J.	233
Bilston, Brian	222
Bird, Mark	144
Blake, William	27
Bleiman, Barbara	199
Booton, Dale	99
Boutris, Despy	58, 204
Brantley, Cal	85
Brodie, Charlie	7
Brontë, Emily	224
Burke, Lucy	208
Burkitt, Carl	81
Castelletti, Charlie	30, 151
Cawood, Aaron	11, 39, 141
Clarke, Emmy	112, 113
Conlon, Dom	87
Cooper, Jack	9
Cope, Wendy	124
Cormack, Annabelle	22, 69

Crane, Stephen   207
Crowell, Grace Noll   93
Day, Kelsey   5
de Keyser, Carmella   94
Dessalines, Cora   180
Dickinson, Emily   36, 84, 168, 177
Dide   35
Dixon, Jo Morris   115
Doyle, Betty   163
Duffy, Carol Ann   13, 15
Dunbar, Paul Laurence   189, 237
Ennis, Stewart   101, 221
Falls, Casper E.   71
Feroze, Jen   227
Finding, Deborah   25
Flanagan, Tom   116
Flo, Lysz   183
Foster, Lois   54, 56
Freeman, Matthew   147
Galef, Daniel   166
García, Clara Elena   201
Gatehouse, Victoria   170
Gibson, Elizabeth   82
Gessler, Christina   211
Giles, Harry Josephine   3, 29

Gill, Nikita	26, 40, 153
Gould, Elizabeth	125
Halabuza, Raye	139, 223
Hardy, Thomas	106
Hardy-Dawson, Sue	157
Hayes, Jer	114
Hennemann, Christina	68
Hughes, Langston	159
Huntsgood, MJ	169
Hutson, Emma	90
Ireton, LJ	37
Jassat, Nadine Aisha	42
Jastrzębska, Maria	126
Jordan, June	28
Knights, Karl	160
Laméris, Danusha	83
Larkin, Philip	21
Lightbown, Stephen	212
Lime, Attie	xix
Linden, Hannah	128
Longfellow, Henry Wadsworth	202
Ly, David	24
MacCaig, Norman	197
McCullough, John	77
Maloku, Dredhëza	108, 190

Moore, Charlotte — 64, 236
Morris, Charlie — 142
Mucha, Laura — 73
Oet, Rainie — 103
Oliver, Mary — 134
O'Rourke, Meghan — 185
Pacton, Jamie — 179
Perron, Lisa Varchol — 123
Perry, Emma — 110
Peters, Sarah — 140
Powell, Eleanor — 213
Renee, Tracie — 43
Robertson, Shauna Darling — 19, 51, 158, 232
Rossetti, Christina — 12, 182, 192
Sami, Annabelle — 172, 234
Saville, Pan — 46
Scalpello, Peter — 104
Schlinkert, Claire — 20
Seigal, Joshua — 216
Stevens, Julie — 92
Stevenson, M. — 173
Stitch, Wilhelmina — 41
Stobierski, Tim — 45
Summers, Aidan — 63
Taylor, Rosamund — 60, 62

Teasdale, Sara   107, 145
Tennyson, Lord Alfred   4
Trommer, Rosemerry Wahtola   89, 148
Waddell, Philip   59
Walton, Rob   52, 230
Wildwood, Raven   225
Williams, Imogen Russell   231
Williams, Kate   203
Wilson, Elspeth   65
Wilson, Robley   10
Winters, Cat   78, 146
Wood, C. T.   187
Woodgate, Harry   132, 149
Woods, Gregory   130
Ziman, Sarah   217

Copyright Acknowledgements

The compiler and publisher would like to thank the following for permission to use their copyrighted material:

Adcock, Fleur: 'Leaving the Tate' from *Collected Poems* (Bloodaxe Books, 2024) © Fleur Adcock. Reproduced with permission of Bloodaxe Books. www.bloodaxebooks.com @bloodaxebooks (twitter/facebook) #bloodaxebooks; **Ahmed, Munira Tabassum:** 'Glossary for Hope' © Munira Tabassum Ahmed. Reprinted with kind permission of author; **Alejandra, Christina:** 'Raw thoughts on 'too much'' © Christina Alejandra. Reprinted with kind permission of author; **Arlett, Megan J.:** 'On Her Fifteenth Birthday, I Tell My Sister Why a Woman is Like a Bouquet of Flowers' © Megan Arlett. Reprinted with kind permission of author; **Bilston, Brian:** 'Message to the 14-Year-Old Me' © Brian Bilston. Reprinted with kind permission of author; **Bird, Mark:** 'Mask' © Mark Bird. Reprinted with kind permission of author; **Bleiman, Barbara:** 'There's No One Else Like Me' © Barbara Bleiman. Reprinted with kind permission of author; **Booton, Dale:** 'The Sunflower Sonnets' © Dale Booton. Reprinted with kind permission of author; **Boutris, Despy:** 'I Want! To Want! To Live!', previous published in *Poet Lore* and 'Age Fourteen, Online Quiz' previously published in *Litmosphere* © Despy Boutris. Reprinted with kind permission of author; **Brantley, Cal:** 'Because the World Didn't End' © Cal Brantley. Reprinted with kind permission of author; **Brodie, Charlie:** 'Two Boys in the Dark' © Charlie Brodie. Reprinted with kind permission of author; **Burke, Lucy:** 'The Bully' © Lucy Burke. Reprinted with kind permission of author; **Burkitt, Carl:** 'Good News' © Carl Burkitt. Reprinted with kind permission of author; **Castelletti, Charlie:** 'Too Angry' and 'Here's what I'm afraid of' © Charlie Castelletti. Reprinted with kind permission of author; **Cawood, Aaron:** 'I Am Trying', 'By-Product' and 'Wreckages' © Aaron Cawood. Reprinted with kind permission of author; **Clarke, Emmy:** 'Later' first published in *in·spire: poems with breath in them* (Fragmented Voices, 2023) and 'Eulogy' first published in *Facing Goodbye* (Wee Sparrow Poetry Press, 2024) © Emmy Clarke. Reprinted with kind permission of author; **Conlon, Dom:** 'The First Cosmonaut' © Dom Conlon. Reprinted with kind permission of author; **Cooper, Jack:** 'The perfect caress has a velocity of three centimetres per second' published by Young Poets

Australia as Edward Cullen takes his shirt off for the twentieth time'. This poem was originally commended in a Young Poets Network challenge and published on the Poetry Society website. It was then published in Elspeth Wilson's pamphlet, *Too Hot to Sleep* (Written Off Publishing, 2023) © Elspeth Wilson. Reprinted with kind permission of author; **Winters, Cat:** 'An Octopus Dwells Inside My Head' and 'Hope' © Cat Winters. Reprinted with kind permission of author; **Wood, C. T.:** 'The Three Deaths'. "This poem was my way of saying goodbye to my grandpa, William "Bill" Wood, or Pop as he was known to me. Until I see him again." © C. T. Wood. Reprinted with kind permission of author; **Woodgate, Harry:** 'What a Joy It Is' and 'if nothing else' © Harry Woodgate. Reprinted with kind permission from author; **Woods, Gregory:** 'The Best Medicine' from *An Ordinary Dog* (Carcanet, 2011) © Gregory Woods. Reprinted by permission of Carcanet. **Ziman, Sarah:** 'Subtext' © Sarah Ziman. Reprinted with kind permission of author.

Acknowledgements

This book would not exist without the encouragement and belief of poetry goddess, colleague, friend and ultimate superstar, Gaby Morgan: thank you for always being an inspiration and, more importantly, a listening ear when I have felt like I'm too much – or not enough. You've always kept me going, and there are no words to describe how grateful I am for it.

Thank you to every single poet who responded to my email, my DM, my online post, and who submitted their work to me – it is always an absolute pleasure reading, compiling and editing your words. It's such an honour to publish you.

Thank you also to every single person behind the scenes: always Rachel Vale, and Arabella Jones, for the beautiful cover design. Thank you to Tanny Hossain for working your admin magic – it's always such a hard task pulling an anthology together, and you're the glue that held this one together! Thank you also to Tracey Ridgewell, Susannah Mason and Amy Boxshall for making this anthology as shiny as possible, as well as the rest of the Macmillan Children's Books team for getting this book into the hands of readers everywhere.